AF708523

God's Healing Dirt

How a Christian Dealt With Depression

Virgil Svendsen

Copyright © 2006 by Virgil Svendsen

All rights reserved. No part of this book shall be reproduced or transmitted in any form or by any means, electronic, mechanical, magnetic, photographic including photocopying, recording or by any information storage and retrieval system, without prior written permission of the publisher. No patent liability is assumed with respect to the use of the information contained herein. Although every precaution has been taken in the preparation of this book, the publisher and author assume no responsibility for errors or omissions. Neither is any liability assumed for damages resulting from the use of the information contained herein.

ISBN 0-7414-3114-9

Published by:

INFINITY
PUBLISHING.COM

1094 New DeHaven Street, Suite 100
West Conshohocken, PA 19428-2713
Info@buybooksontheweb.com
www.buybooksontheweb.com
Toll-free (877) BUY BOOK
Local Phone (610) 941-9999
Fax (610) 941-9959

Printed in the United States of America

Printed on Recycled Paper

Published May 2006

TABLE OF CONTENTS

FOREWORD

BY: JARED SVENDSEN

When I first read this book, I was very much surprised by the content. For the first 30 years of my life, I knew only half of his story. I had always known my father as the strong leader of our family. He was invincible. I really didn't worry too much growing up because I knew that my dad would take care of any problem that might threaten my little world.

Dad loved Mom. That was one of the fundamental axioms of life. That love was as constant as the sun coming up or brushing my teeth before bed. That love provided the security that encompassed me in the final minutes before falling to sleep each night.

Dad loved Joey and me. There was absolutely never any doubt in my mind about that. He spent countless hours helping me with school projects, taking me to soccer practice and instructing me on how to improve my lay ups. He was a faithful TV buddy. He would sit through cartoon after cartoon with me because I asked him too—for some reason it just wasn't the same without him. He raised me to be a diehard Clemson football fan and to admire Larry Bird's jump shot. And he punished me when my rebellious deeds called for it.

From an early age, I understood that there were consequences resulting from my actions. Best of all, he was just there.

Dad loved Jesus. The greatest thing that my father ever did was to teach me the love of Christ. Together with my mother, they laid for me a strong spiritual foundation upon which I could grow as a Christian. I am very blessed. I have an earthly father whose example of love helped me to grasp the nature of my Heavenly Father's love for me. He took God's wonderful gift of fatherhood seriously, understanding the gravity of his responsibility. His walk with Jesus will be indelibly marked in my mind. The pattern of his commitment to Christ has been adopted by my soul. Dad showed me the way to eternal life.

That's the only story I knew. The man being described by my father throughout this book seemed to me like a fictional character out of some Kafka book. How could I be living in the same house for all those years with a man suffering so deeply and not know? An even better question: How could I be living in the same house for all those years with a man suffering so deeply and only see a father with love for his family and a deep, joyful devotion to his Creator?

The answer to those questions is the crux of this book. Many people go through their entire lives only knowing half of the story. Unfortunately, they only know the ugly, oppressive chapters of depression and spiritual captivity. Whether you are plagued by depression or some other spiritual, mental or physical "thorn"; God so wants to reveal Himself to you. Through God's gift of grace, we can be totally transformed. We can be totally new creations. We don't have to be a slave to our pathetic earthly nature. Instead, we can live victoriously in the knowledge of God's healing power. Despite Virgil's struggles, he lived a life that boldly proclaimed God's conquest over his depression. Throughout my life, I only saw Dad as the champion that God called him to be!

My father is a new creation and has been for the last 25 years. His life is a testimony to the human condition. We are all physical beings. Consequently, we are all heirs to Adam's curse to suffer under the weight of our physical imperfections and the hostile attacks from our enemy. But most importantly, my dad's life is a testimony to God's saving grace. Almighty God provides temporary physical relief through his miraculous "healing dirt". He provides spiritual relief through His Living Word. Finally, God provides the ultimate remedy: everlasting life with Him through the blood of His Son's sacrificial death. The message in this book is a powerful one. Through his experience with depression and his relationship with God, Virgil is able to offer a clear message of hope and redemption. This book is not filled with empty words of conjecture or theory. These are the words of a man tried by fire and victorious to the end.

FOREWORD
BY: JOEY SVENDSEN

Walking into the living room (Feb 94) as a 16 year-old boy with tears in my eyes, I interrupted my parents' movie with sobs. I had been spending the past 30 minutes in my bedroom, pleading to God to get my life straightened out, obsessing over the words that I carefully articulated to Him, and dreadfully doubting that He was even paying attention.

From this early age, as I fought for sanity and peace-of-mind, I mistook my battles as mere spiritual struggles that I was determined to get myself through. I needed to be a better person, I needed to be more committed, more passionate, I needed to strengthen my faith, and stop disappointing God. If I could do all this, I just knew I would earn a sound mind.

My parents had other thoughts on the matter. You see, around 15 years prior, my dad had similar experiences, and this was all too familiar to them: the moping around, the obsessive thoughts and worries, the sadness. There was no doubt to them that I was experiencing a chemical imbalance or depression if you will. They encouraged me to seek medical attention and perhaps start taking medicine for my depression.

Unfortunately, I just couldn't see it. These feelings of fear, worry, and hopelessness had become my way of life. They were what I was used to. I was even able to go around them and still enjoy some aspects of life. For these feelings to be anything out of the ordinary, such as depression (oh my gosh, no!), didn't make any sense to me at all.

Until 1998, during my junior year of college, I sat on my worn, beaten up couch and evaluated my most recent episode of mental trauma. I started to realize (by God's grace) that these thoughts I had were very abnormal. They were not the result of typical college trials, but the result of an unhealthy mind.

As I called my parents to discuss this, it led to some visits to the doctor, which led to trying different medications to help me with my depression. It was a much longer, more dreadful, heart-wrenching process than I expected or that I could have ever imagined. Nothing worked. I tried one medication after another, but to no avail. I was doomed. This brought me to one conclusion. I have no choice than to believe and act on the words that I've heard and believed my whole life: Jesus Christ is all I need.

I began to pray more. I began to read my Bible not just as a daily chore, but as an act of desperation. My faith became way more than just what I was brought up in. It became my only hope. I always believed what the Bible said, but now I was forced to believe on my own behalf in order to drag me out of my hell.

Days turned into weeks, and weeks in to months. Sometimes, I felt like God was helping me. Other times, I felt like He was hiding His face from me or that He perhaps didn't even exist. However, I did not have a choice but seek harder, to press on, and to believe what I've always been taught and what I always assumed to be true. If this was not the answer, so be it. But I had to believe. I had nothing else. Jesus has to love me. God has to exist. He has to care. I continued to read His word and seek answers fervently as I became more numb and more dead to the world.

As a young boy obeys his mom by drinking his orange juice for his sore throat, I continued to obey my Heavenly father by believing that this Jesus Christ (His Son) was not only the hope of the world, but also the only hope for me. As a young boy is unaware of the vitamin C cleansing his body, giving it strength to fight off the sickness, I was unaware that the Bread of Life was cleansing my Spirit, giving me strength to live by His Spirit.

More time went by and the depression lingered, but I was learning day by day the most important lesson that I would learn in my life: Jesus Christ was the answer and that He was all I needed. The words that I had passively believed were becoming my way of life. They were becoming my way of thinking. They were precisely becoming my only hope. It wasn't until three years later, as a married man and a teacher of 4 years, that God led me to an effective medication to remedy my depression.

However, the damage had been done. Or shall I say, God's glory was accomplished. These difficult times transformed me in to a man that was solely dependent on God. I was a man, now believing, that if everything that I held dear was stripped away from me in a blink of an eye, I would be okay. This transformation was the result of me experiencing a Father that allowed His son to walk through the fires and the high waters (while He held my hand) to show me that He was truly my answer. He loved me and wanted me to take any hope that I had in my life and all the frivolous jewels that my life was offering me and trade it for a solid, never-ending, loving, secure relationship with Him, my Creator.

My days of depression are behind me now. Occasionally, I will have a bad day or two that take me back a little to those days of horror. But, my hope is rested on Jesus Christ and Him alone will I trust. I always know that He will continue to walk me through these days.

Looking back on 1993, how my perception of God has changed. I don't have to perfectly articulate my words. God created me and knows my thoughts. I don't have to straighten out my life. Jesus already did that on the cross. I know that everything rests in His hands now: my body, my mind, and praise God, my soul.

As you read my dad's book, you have the opportunity to read, in way more depth, about another battle with depression and how he found, too, that the only answers to survive were in the words of Jesus.

Romans 8:28 rings true through all of this. All things work for the good for those who love the Lord. I am thankful for one good work in particular that came out of my dad's struggles in that he was able to assist me in my battle. I could tell my dad about the insane thoughts I was having and they weren't insane to him in the least! He instilled in me the knowledge of antidepressants being miracles of God and that they were nothing to be ashamed of. I needed to hear this, because at one point, I was convinced that God was going to heal me without medication. He taught me that a depressed mind is similar to a sore throat or a cancerous stomach. It needed to be dealt with not just through prayer, but also through medication and a doctor's supervision.

The most important good work that came through our depression was that my dad and I are forever changed. Our depression has changed us and made us stronger men of God. I know that the both of us would not trade that for anything in the world.

Then he spat on the ground and made mud from the spittle and smoothed it over the blind man's eyes and told him, "Go and wash in the Pool of Siloam" (the word "Siloam" means "Sent"). So the man went where he was sent and washed and came back seeing!

John 9:6,7

CHAPTER 1

MY STRUGGLE

"And the Word was made Flesh and Dwelt Among Us".[1] *John 1:14.* Thirty years ago I couldn't imagine how important these words would be to me, and innumerable other scriptures, and words of knowledge from the Holy Spirit. Millions of our fellow strugglers with depression and other forms of affliction would testify that because they did not lose their hope in God or His promises, they were able to keep going step by step-or sometimes inch by inch.[2] I don't understand how anyone makes it through life without God's Word. This man certainly couldn't. I'm just an average guy, not a guy that would stand out at all in a crowd. I guess to understand where I am, you'd have to know a little about where I've been.

I don't remember much of my first three years, but I do remember catching bumble bees in a jelly jar amidst the clover blossoms where we lived in downtown Charleston, S.C. I remember my dad and me shrimping with drop nets off of my Uncle Virgil's dock on James Island. Around five years of age I can remember kindergarten and taking naps, going to the doctor and getting shots and being scared of Santa Claus. The nuns that taught me in first and second grade are remembered as kind but strict and they taught me about God from the Baltimore Catechism. I can remember my dad taking me to the circus when I was about 5 or 6, I think. I remember it was a three-ring circus, because I kept trying to see what was going on in all of the rings, but couldn't and it was frustrating. My dad was a big kidder. I had very curly blond hair, and once him and mom put a little dress on me just for fun. I have a picture of me in it, so it's not just a cute story. Supposedly the little girls in the neighborhood were jealous of me and my curly hair, one even going so far as to hit me in the head with a roller skate.

When I was a little kid I heard my mom and dad talk about someone that had had a nervous breakdown. As I grew older I understood that these people got very sad, very suddenly and that normally they would never be quite the same. Also I learned that these people were subject to having more nervous breakdowns. I now realize that these people were probably suffering from depression. My grandmother had two brothers, one of which fought in World War I, and they were lifelong alcoholics. The one that didn't serve could not do so because his brother had chopped four toes off of one of his feet on a dare. I really believe that they suffered from depression. Although I knew that depressed people were sad, I had no way of knowing the intenseness, the mental anguish and the concentrated pain that clinically depressed people experience. No one really can unless they've experienced it. I do remember that there were times as a young teenager that I really felt sad, and for no reason, really. Back then I just thought I had the "blues" or that I was "down in the dumps".

Depression up until the last 20–25 years was not something discussed; you just didn't bring it up. It was hush-hush much like an out of wedlock pregnancy. It was much too embarrassing for the family and the depressed family member and this was sad because medical treatment has been available at least since the 1950's. In my own case, I didn't want anyone to know out of embarrassment and fear that I might lose my job. For some reason the general consensus was that the sufferer could get "un-depressed" if they really just tried hard. "Come on Jim, snap out of it. Grow up. You're just being a big baby. Snap out of it." That might work after a short time for 'situational' depression or sadness from a broken relationship or bad business decision or the like. Sufferers of clinical depression are not so fortunate. These sufferers, as I found out need medical treatment and to my great benefit, much more.

As a small child going to Catholic elementary school, at times I would get obsessed with dread over sinning. This was good in a way as it kept me out of trouble most of the time, and maintain my status as a good boy. But looking back, I can see that I was a little troubled. It seemed to me that God was just waiting to get me, and that I might miss out on heaven. This wasn't taught but it's how my mind was wired. A guilt complex is probably the label you'd put on my neurosis. A little boy doesn't get that messed up that fast without some kind of problem.

Remember to emphasize God's loving nature as well as His just nature. Your kids need to know that at an early age. I remember as I was receiving communion one Sunday, I dropped the wafer on the floor. I was so sure that I couldn't be forgiven for this sacrilege. I was perceived by the nuns that taught me as a very good little boy and they were already grooming me to be a priest by the time I was 10. A dorky little kid and a bit of a goody-goody little kid was probably how you would describe me. The nuns would also get me to lead the class in the Stations of the Cross at church, and I'd be pretty nervous. Prayer at home was of the memorized type (Now I lay me down to sleep…), and Catholics were not encouraged to read the Bible, so no knowledge from there. We did have a huge Bible that sat on the coffee table though.

CHAPTER 2

ANXIETY

I realize now reflecting back on days gone by that I have always lived with some anxiety, sometimes bad and sometimes not so bad. I know now that anxiety is extremely common; it's estimated that about 13% of the United States population has anxiety. Anxiety disorder affects all ages, including teens and children. I just coped with mine, sort of accepting the fact that I wasn't as good as most other kids, somehow defective. For example, I didn't stick up for myself much when I was a little kid. I started doing that when I got to be a teenager. I felt a lot more confident as a teen, but I was still petrified to give speeches in front of my class, but a lot of people are wired like that; and have feelings of intense stress, worry, fear and panic. The important thing is to realize that the anxiety can be treated and that living with constant anxiety is not necessary.

What causes anxiety? There is no one cause for anxiety; it's likely that many factors contribute to a person's chance of developing anxiety. Scientists have broken down the potential causes into three groups, genetics and early learning, brain biochemistry and the "fight or flight" mechanism.

Neurotransmitters are chemical messengers in the brain that regulate a person's thoughts or feelings. Sometimes there is a problem with the way the brain's messages are sent due to a chemical imbalance. Two of the primary neurotransmitters that affect a person's feelings are serotonin and dopamine. When there is an imbalance of these chemicals, a person can feel depressed or anxious.

Anxiety disorders tend to run in families, so if a person's mom or dad, or other close relative has anxiety; they have a higher chance of developing anxiety themselves. Growing up in a family where fear and anxiety are constantly shown to children by role models can "teach" them to be anxious as well. In addition, if a child grows up in an abusive home, he or she may learn to always expect the worse.[1] I wasn't in a physically abusive home, but that certainly describes me.

Strict was the word for my dad and it served me well in a lot of ways. Barbara would tell me that she would sit behind me, my brother and my dad at Mass on Sunday, and she could not believe how disciplined we were. She said that we would not look to the side for a minute we were always looking straight ahead, and didn't utter a peep. My brother and I knew that we would really get it when we got home if we misbehaved.

I had a good childhood and knew that I was very well cared for. My dad always made sure that we went on summer vacations, which we looked forward to with great anticipation. My dad was an orphan at age nine and he lost his dad in 1918 at age one month. He was passed around from one uncle to another before he was sent to the orphanage in Raleigh, North Carolina. When his uncle told him that he was going to have to be sent to an orphanage, my dad begged him not to put him in the Charleston Orphanage because it would be embarrassing. This was because his friends would know that he had family in Charleston that would not keep him. His uncles were strict disciplinarians; and I guess that's where he got his stern ways. I seemed to have inherited most of my mom's personality. She was very quiet and reserved and a sensor, feeler kind of person yet very strong. My dad was a tough guy, who suffered from ulcers and the loss of two fingers and use of one in a work-related accident. He never showed his emotions and I never saw him cry, up until he was about 80 years old. He had a temper at times and could be very harsh. I think he shaped my vision of how a man was supposed to handle himself, but I must admit I didn't know if I could measure up. In my mind I didn't think that I did.

It is true now but even more so in the past that some men prefer to develop socially acceptable stress-related illnesses such as ulcers, than to have it known that they have sought professional help for depression. Other masks of masculine melancholy include difficulty forming intimate relationships, abusive behavior and rage.

Research also shows a genetic predisposition for a chemical imbalance in people with anxiety. Since the structure of the brain and its processes are inherited, this is yet another reason why anxiety can run in families.

Changing the way we think can mean attempting to undo years of thought patterns. Some of these thought patterns can be negative and automatic. It's been a lifelong journey for me. One of the things that I hope to accomplish by writing this book is to shorten that learning curve for as many people as possible. It doesn't have to be life-long, although I wouldn't trade my journey for anything. I don't just have life now. I have abundant life and eternal life.

When a person senses danger, the body prepares itself to either fight (defend itself) or flee (run away from the situation). The body's fight or flight mechanism causes the body's heart rate to increase, eyes to dilate, and the body to prepare itself for a dangerous situation. Theses responses allow a person to protect him/herself. Even though these responses are intended to be a good thing, sometimes the body misunderstands a situation, and believes that there is danger when in reality there is not (taking a test, giving a speech, etc.) There is a part of the brain called the amygdale that triggers the fight or flight response. This part of the brain is trained to remember the last thing that triggered the fight or flight mechanism (taking a test or giving a speech). This is the brain's attempt to protect the body from future danger by keeping track of all things that might cue danger. Even though this part of the brain is trying to protect a person, it can be the cause of much unnecessary anxiety. The brain has to be "un-trained" not to react in fight or flight to something that is not actually dangerous.

A phobia is similar. A specific phobia is an intense fear of something that has little or no actual danger. Some of the more common specific phobias are closed-in places, heights, escalators, tunnels, highway driving, water, flying, dogs and injuries involving blood. But the list is endless.

Another disorder is Obsessive Compulsive Disorder (OCD). OCD is characterized by obsessions and compulsions that are time-consuming, distressing and interfere with normal routine relationships, and daily activities. This can be excessive washing of hands, constantly checking the locks on the doors and windows or similar actions.

Post Traumatic Stress Disorder (PTSD) is a debilitating condition that can develop following a terrifying event. Often, people with PTSD have persistent frightening thoughts and memories of the ordeal and feel emotionally numb. Many war veterans experience this and although I am a Viet-Nam war veteran, I didn't suffer from this; however I did suffer from regrets of something I did that was very stupid and something that really bothered me for a long time.

Anxiety can affect many aspects of a person's life. If someone is always worried or anxious, it is doubtful that he/she can fully enjoy life. Anxiety might affect one's ability to make new friends, perform well at work, and try new things.

Sometimes people who suffer from anxiety revert to alcohol or drug abuse. Using drugs or alcohol to treat anxiety is extremely dangerous and could make anxiety much worse and cause other serious health problems. That is one thing I was determined not to do…turn to alcohol. I didn't even think about illegal drugs. I wanted to get back to normal.

Physically, constant anxiety can cause problems with eating and sleeping habits, and prolonged anxiety may lead to more serious health problems. Finding the right treatment can help a person break free from anxiety and live life to the fullest.[2]

As a little kid, teenager and young adult, I never had constant or prolonged anxiety, but I do believe I had a social anxiety disorder. The unifying characteristic in social anxiety disorder is a fear of performing poorly in social situations and suffering from embarrassment or humiliation. By definition, social situations mean interacting with or performing for other people and being under their potential scrutiny. Social anxiety extends beyond shyness; it can limit the social lives, education and even the career choices of those who suffer from it. I remember dreading for months and months the prospect of giving a speech, although not constantly.

As I grew older and entered high school, I lost most of my spiritual concerns and became aware that I was very shy and found it hard to be gregarious. I was very much an introvert, but I still had a lot of friends. I did assert myself to a degree and got into a fight with a bully that thought I'd be easy prey. I escaped with cuts under my eye and he left jiggling some loose teeth. I went out for junior varsity football and track, and did well at practices as a smallish linebacker. Unfortunately, I didn't make the team so I went out for track and ran the half mile and mile and I did very well at practices, but at the first tri-meet, which did not count as a regular season meet, I wasn't put in one single event. (So much for sports.) I did well academically, however, even becoming president of JETS (Junior Engineering Technical Society) and went to college and received a degree in Civil Engineering. Before I forget, I became aware that I had this overall feeling that happiness and contentment were just around the corner. After high school, I thought that when I made it out of college, that would be the gateway to utopia. Boy was I wrong. At orientation we were told that one in three of us would not graduate. My first year and a half, I struggled to stay above a 2.0. For financial reasons and a desire to prevent myself from getting drafted out of college, I took advanced ROTC my junior and senior years. Between 1965 and 1969 guys were getting drafted out of college. So I was all set to be a commissioned officer in the Army when I graduated. A few things happened to me in 1969 that would have a great impact on the rest of my life, one positive and one negative. One afternoon I began to have an excruciating pain in my back and side. My roommate wasn't around, and I didn't leave a note because I thought I'd be down to the infirmary and right back. When I walked into the infirmary, the nurse looked at me and told me that I was white as a sheet. Nausea came over me like a wave. The diagnosis after some tests and xrays was kidney stones. This was something I'd never even heard of. After a few days of Demerol and straining my urine, I gave birth to a jagged little kidney stone. The doctor said that this could be a one-time deal or this could be the beginning of a lifetime of forming kidney stones. I had rarely ever been sick or seen a doctor, much less been in the hospital, so I was quite bothered having to miss classes. My friends brought some of my books which helped me from falling too far behind, which I was very much afraid of.

On a couple of occasions, I abused alcohol; I think once over a girl and a couple of times because I had to study when just about everyone else was at a dance or a party. My major and my limited intellect required that I studied my tail off to get and maintain my stellar 2.3 GPR. No one would accuse me of being a big socializer.

Romans 8:28 – "All things work together for good for those that love the Lord and are called according to His purpose"[3]

This scripture didn't apply to me at the time because I definitely was not living for God, and I really just had a knowledge of God and rudimentary at that. The only bible I had ever seen or opened was a huge red leather bible that sat on the coffee table. It was a Catholic bible because it had pictures of Mass and explained the various sacraments. My religious upbringing was all Catholic and early training was out of the Baltimore Catechism, a publication that presented the Catholicism's basic precepts. My relationship with God was not a deep personal relationship, but one of great fear. I regained my spiritual awareness in college. My expectation was for God to clobber me when I made the wrong move. During college, I walked to Mass every Sunday and I wanted to remain in good standing with God. I thought that it was very important, because I wanted to go to heaven. I wouldn't do anything to offend God and was very disturbed whenever someone made fun of God or spoke disparagingly about Him or spiritual things. I didn't like being around that sort of thing. I felt like a lightning bolt could come out of the sky and zap somebody or maybe something worse, but I didn't like it. I wasn't a party animal, in fact I was looking for a good girl that was more on the reserved side and a girl with similar religious values would be a must. I was a religious, person that prayed and had an obsessive respect for God. That's a good thing though.

I think maybe I felt that I had to appease God through my religion, but I now know that what is needed is Faith that confronts and conquers. (Hebrews 11:30-40)[4] I didn't know much about faith, except that believing in God was like breathing and I attribute that to my Catholic upbringing and the wonderful nuns that taught me through the years. In my very younger years the nuns or sisters as we called them, had me pegged to be a priest. When I started to notice girls I knew that was not an option.

Religion focuses on the past where Faith sees the now. (Romans 8:1, Hebrews 11:1)[5]

Religion focuses on form where Faith has substance. (Hebrews 11:1)6

Religion feeds the flesh, Faith strengthens the spirit. (Romans 8:1)7

Looking back I guess I can remember that there were many times that I felt melancholy, but it was very temporary and not debilitating and I must have just figured that all kids must feel like this sometimes. Times of boredom or disappointment were times that I remember feeling very sad and the older that I got, the more I was aware of it. I remember feeling that if I could just get to the point where I had no worries or responsibilities, I'd feel happy and every day would feel like a Saturday morning watching cartoons. Oh I knew I'd have to get a job and work like everyone else but, I thought that at least I wouldn't have anything hanging over my head, like college and then military service. I always thought that my depression was attributable to the circumstances of life; I didn't know anything about chemical imbalances.

I had dated some but never found the girl that was right for me. I had a couple of close relationships, but I always ended up disenchanted or dissed. I remember telling my mom that I was giving up on women and that I didn't think I'd ever find one that I loved. Looking back on it, there was probably a little depression there, but I didn't think of it that way. I thought I was just getting tough and cynical. In many ways I thought of myself as someone who could take just about anything and that I should be that way, because that was being a real man. Everything was tolerable and everything could be toughed out.

Positively in the year of 1969, I met Barbara. She was dating a friend of mine and he asked her to get a date for me. She knew me from school and would sometimes sit behind me at Mass. I barely talked to my date. She got a little irritated with me. Barbara and I just hit it off great. It was practically love at first site for me. Her reputation as a good and pure girl preceded her, and I had given up on ever finding such a girl. We both fell in love within months. Was I ecstatic or what? The girl of my dreams agreed to marry me. It seemed God was blessing me, without me hardly giving Him a thought. I was very scared of Him, but it was a reverent fear, and I had no close relationship with Him.

That summer I did my basic training at Fort Bragg, which was one hot place. There was a lot of camaraderie and I made some good friends there. I teamed up with a guy for the Orienteering competition which combined the abilities to use a map and compass with the ability to run. We did very well and came in second in our Company. We crawled under barbed wire while live ammunition was fired over our head, qualified with the M-16, learned how to throw hand grenades and fire mortars, and make battlefield decisions.

Again my happiness had to be put on hold as I had a two year commitment to Uncle Sam. So I was off to Fort Belvoir, Fort Leonard Wood (Fort Lost in the Woods) we called it and Fort Benjamin Harrison for training and duty. At Fort Leonard Wood, I was told that there was a need at Fort Benjamin Harrison for three officers to inspect construction being accomplished by reservists. As I made the drive from Missouri to Indiana, I started feeling a little gloomy. By the time I arrived and was in the waiting room preparing to meet the base Commander I sensed a dark, gloomy cloud come over me. I felt totally lost, totally incapable and I knew I had a long road ahead, just barely into my two year active duty commitment to the Army with one year ahead somewhere else in the world besides the USA. I didn't have any experience in leading men, at least not much. The other two officers were married so I didn't really have a buddy to pal around with, but they would have me over for cookouts on the weekends sometimes and one of them had a little daughter named Susie that was fun to be around. We would all three play basketball against other trios on base and were pretty hard to beat. I had a pretty good jump shot, stuck to my man like glue and was pretty good at finding the open teammate. I prided myself in sticking my man so that he was lucky if he ever got the ball.

By this time Barbara and I were engaged. The base commander had a party at his house, and of course he invited us lieutenants. Things were going okay until the general's niece or daughter showed up, I can't remember now. She had her own car and wanted me to leave the party and go out with her. I turned her down, and I think it must have really hurt her feelings. The following Monday, my commanding officer called me in and said that the base commander was not happy that his niece got rejected. In fact, he questioned, "What's the matter with him? Any red-blooded American boy would have gone out with her". I exploded and was going to go see the general, but my CO ordered me to stop and ordered me not to speak to him about it. I settled down but I wasn't happy. But you see, I was engaged and there was no way I would do that as an engaged man. The first year commitment was stateside but the second year was overseas, and as luck would have it, (actually God allowed it for my ultimate good), I was given my assignment, the Republic of Viet-Nam. This separation was the most difficult period in my life up to that time, another knockdown in the brawl I was in.

I was actually proud to serve my country in this way. I knew my dad would be proud of me and maybe I would have some war stories of my own. I wasn't wishing for any just trying to be realistic. But it was another hard separation, another postponement of our wedding. But I think to some degree my depression may have lifted a little as I found some pride in serving my country in a war where people were getting killed. Barbara cried and my mom cried as the day came to fly. As I watched Barbara's house receding in my rear-view mirror, I wondered if I'd ever see it again. I'm not being melodramatic, that's just how my dark mood was in those days. Bouncing over the Pacific Ocean to Hawaii and to Okinawa and finally to my destination of Viet-Nam, I wondered the same kind of dark thoughts. I wondered to myself, "Will I be making the return trip?" Over there I got my assignment, Can Tho in the Mekong Delta where I was a construction platoon leader. The Colonel in charge of assignments asked me if I had a preference, Saigon or Can Tho in the Delta. I tried to be as casual as I could when I responded. The Colonel said, "Can Tho, huh? That's what I thought, but you're going to the Delta!" It almost seemed like he was snickering. My college buddy got duty in Saigon. He said that when I came out of the Colonel's office the look on my face and it's paleness left no doubt in his mind where I was going.

When I arrived in the Delta, the place smelled like an open sewer, and for good reason – it was. The villagers cooked, bathed, washed dishes and clothes and urinated and defecated all in the same little ditches that were always near. Their toilets consisted of little wooden platforms built on rickety poles over the ditches and gullies, but usually these were ten to twenty feet off of the road as to afford some privacy. But there were no sides on the "toilets". My duties were to build a concrete pier/steel stringer bridge, run a rock quarry, build roads and pour concrete slabs for whatever. The bridge site was 20 miles from the nearest friendly troops in Can Tho so we were also assigned the task of defending our position. Now I realize that there were periods of time over there that I was depressed, but I dismissed it as temporary sadness and that everything would be alright. Barbara and I wrote every day, but sometimes the mail would be delayed and we wouldn't here from each other for a week. I was scared she had found someone a little closer to home.

My platoon and I were fired upon a few times, machine gun and mortar fire and on one occasion, many of my men were wounded some seriously. On another occasion, the morning after an identical attack, you could smell death coming from the banks of the creek over which we were building the bridge. Marines were brought in to sweep the area and found the remains of over fifty Viet Cong. I didn't get a scratch. I got to assist a general in passing out some purple hearts, though. We found out later that our interpreter who strangely disappeared after that assault was actually an enemy combatant. I felt a strong compassion for my men and visited a couple that were more seriously wounded and required hospitalization. It sounds a little strange to say "my men", because I was only twenty - three or twenty - four myself. I say this because even though I did not know the Lord as my Savior, I was a "decent" person that cared about others. However, I still cared more about me and what was going on in my little life.

My men had all sorts of problems. A few were heavy drug users, two were so messed up that I had to send them back to battalion headquarters in Can Tho. One blew the eardrums out of a woman by firing a pistol near her ear. Some of the nearby villagers wanted to take him by force and do him bodily harm. I had to promise them that he would be gone by the next day. The other had a mental breakdown because I didn't know that it was his birthday. He believed that it was traditional to get a day off on your birthday and that I should have known it. He let me know his displeasure in no uncertain terms. In fact, I was the worst platoon leader that he ever had. One of my sergeants went AWOL and I had to give him an Article 15, a disciplinary action that included some loss of pay. He was a habitual alcoholic. One young man wanted to go home because his wife was going to leave him. I tried to facilitate getting him some time to go home but couldn't.

Little kids were always getting run over by army vehicles. I sat on a court martial with two other officers, in the case of a young dump truck driver who was going about fifty-five through a village while intoxicated, killing a little boy. The case was dismissed because no one checked to see if he was dead prior to burying him. Sounds crazy!? It's true. The kids were pretty friendly over there. They didn't resent us being there like many of the adults. Some of the adults didn't really care which side won, they would make money off of whoever was in residence. One thing about the kids, you did not want to buy these things from them that they called "Kool Pops". They looked refreshing but they would give you the worst case of diarrhea. Thankfully, I don't know that from experience, I was warned ahead of time.

I had to go to Saigon once to deliver some mail to two of my men that were incarcerated, and while I was there I looked up my college buddy. It was good to reconnect and he took me by to see another classmate of ours. It was then that I learned that one of our Civil Engineering classmates was killed in action earlier that month leaving behind a wife. Although Barbara and I were tempted once to get married before I left I was determined not to allow the possibility that she become a widow. I don't say this to sound noble, it's just the truth. I didn't want it to be any more difficult for her. I wanted her to be free and clear to marry and be happy. I was content to just be a fading memory, if it came to that as long as she could be happy.

All of these kind of events, I think helped to mask my undiagnosed depression, which had not yet reached critical mass. Also the thought and anticipation of coming home helped overcome the waves of depression as well. I was in the up cycle of, "Well I'll be happy when I finally…". It was always something just around the corner that was going to make me happy.

It was an exhilarating moment when the plane lifted off the runway and we were all headed for home. We actually got delayed about six hours because the compound was mortared.

What a happy homecoming. I couldn't eat on the plane. As I walked down the ramp and headed toward the terminal, there was my mom greeting me with a big hug followed closely by Barbara and Dad. Happiness was finally within my grasp. I had to get a job though. As I had worked several summers with the South Carolina Highway Department, I quickly got a job with them, making a decent salary. Things were falling into place.

My happiness was secured on November 25, 1971, when I married Barbara Elaine Craven. I showed up at the church about 4 hours early – I didn't want to be late. She was so beautiful inside and out and still is. My mom said that it was a marriage made in heaven and indeed it was. We were so much alike, very "religious", non-partiers, that preferred to be alone most of the time just enjoying being together. We weren't together except for short periods during our more than 2 year courtship. We had no problems, life couldn't get any better, or so I thought, but it could get worse, as I was about to find out.

The non- specific uretheritis came back and it was very troubling to me. Doctors could find nothing at all. They didn't find the two large kidney stones in my right kidney. It would have been better if they could have found something, something to treat, but they didn't. Doctors aren't perfect and medicine isn't an exact science. I actually had had a kidney stone while I was in basic training at Fort Bragg, but I didn't think that what I was going through was related. I look back now and I see that this medical problem was a threat to my happiness, and it bothered me for about a year from the fall of 1972 to the winter of 1973. I didn't realize it, but I was reaching a critical mass for an emotional breakdown. Now believe me, I know that my problem was very insignificant compared to what many people go through and do not fall apart, but my lurking depression was compounding my problems.

This condition would go away for a little while, and then it would come back, and this cycle continued for about a year. I remember developing a fear of it coming back each time that it would go away. I didn't know exactly what caused it or how to prevent it. Always in the back of my mind was the question, "Am I going to have this problem my whole life?"

So many things were going on that I thought I

was in some kind of brawl. I'd get knocked down, and then get back up and get knocked down again. Every time I'd say to myself, "You have to be strong". So by my own strength I would drag myself back into the fight and plow ahead.

"Depression can come on after multiple episodes of emotional trauma, and can be linked to circumstances. It can also be linked to unmet emotional needs while growing up, it may have spiritual roots, or it may be primarily a biological illness that is genetically inherited. Most often these causes overlap. The most effective treatment for depression, regardless of its cause (or overlapping causes) is a cooperative, multidisciplinary effort that considers all areas of a depressed person's life – emotional, relational, spiritual and physical.

All of us have a certain vulnerability to depression. Given the right kind of stress, the right magnitude of stress, and the right duration of stress, it is possible, perhaps even normal, for anyone to become depressed to some degree."[8]

God allowed me to see that I could not be self-reliant. He wanted me to see that apart from Him I can do nothing and that I needed to trust Him in absolutely everything, even in His provisions for healing.

In late 1973, I had a flare-up of non-specific

uretheritis. It was the straw that broke the camel's back and I spiraled into the pit of clinical depression. At first I wallowed in it in self-pity, but then when I tried to get out of it, I couldn't. It was as if the parking brake of my mind was set in the emotional gear of sadness and hopelessness. Then real panic set in. Never had I experienced anything that I couldn't control.

If I had had any real spiritual foundation, I would have had somewhere to start, some refuge, but I had none. Of course I found out later that this was a physical condition. Try as I might, I could not push this "thing" out of my mind. Hopelessness set in even deeper. There were no plans for the future, no looking forward to anything. None of the things that I used to enjoy interested me anymore; I was really consumed by depression. I felt very isolated from everyone, so alone and I really felt separated from myself in many ways. I viewed my life from the outside like watching a movie. Making the situation even worse was what I knew it was doing to Barbara. She didn't have a husband anymore, no one to share the good things of life. She had to look at my long face everyday and know that I was pretending to be fine when we were around other people. Amazingly to me she didn't leave me, didn't give up on me, she actually still loved me.

Depression is not the same thing as having

the "blues" or feeling sad every once in awhile – and then bouncing back to your old self. Depression can be mild, moderate or so bad that it affects every part of your life – your body, your thoughts, your feelings and your behavior. It can have an impact on your family relationships, your friendships and your ability to work, play or just get through the day. At its worst, depression can make you feel like you don't want to live. These thoughts and feelings are not your fault – they can be part of depression.

When the sadness continues or keeps returning, when everyday things like sleeping or spending time with your family and simply enjoying life continue to be difficult, what you are feeling is just not "the blues". My most significant symptoms were feelings of worthlessness, hopelessness and guilt.

Please don't wait to get medical help. Depression can be treated and you can feel better.

CHAPTER 3

WHAT CAUSES DEPRESSION?

Due to the complexity of depression, an exact cause has yet to be determined. Researchers have narrowed down possibilities and conclude that depression may be caused by chemical imbalance, genetic factors, psychological predisposition, physical factors and environmental stresses.

Depression often runs in families. This has led researchers to believe that there may be a genetic link. Sometimes depression can occur in generation after generation of a particular family. Other times, however there appears to be no genetic link. Researchers conclude that while you are more likely to develop depression if another family member has the disorder, signs of depression may appear in instances where it has not presented itself in any other family member. "This inherited depression is often more severe than other types of depression and less responsive to social support, psychotherapy, or spiritual forms of treatment. In persons biologically predisposed to depression - including the most devout believers – a small error in judgment, a slight indiscretion, or a minor interpersonal conflict may trigger a full-blown depressive episode.

When this happens to believers, no matter how much they pray, go to church or read their Bible, they still suffer from depression. No matter how much they confess their sins, treat others kindly or "lay down their lives for God," they still remain depressed. Standing in judgment of such persons only intensifies their pain, making matters worse for all concerned. However, encouragement, support and assistance in pursuing every available avenue of treatment can help alleviate their pain."[1]

Scientists believe that there may be a link between depression and a certain psychological predisposition for negativity. People who have low self-esteem, a negative attitude and an overall pessimistic view of life are more likely to exhibit signs of depression. "These individuals exhibit a persistent inability to appreciate the positive aspects of life along with an almost obsessive preoccupation with the negative. A contributing factor to this low self-esteem and negative attitude appears to be the experience of major losses during childhood or early deprivation of emotional needs. For example, marital, job-related or other significant stresses may distract parents from a child during a critical developmental period."[2] Depression is more likely to occur in people who are easily overwhelmed by stress. To me this emphasizes the importance of how you raise your children and how important it is for them to grow up in a loving family, where there is a mom and dad who show there love for them. "Regardless of the circumstances, the way to wholeness is not through blaming or bitterness, but rather through forgiveness, the release of long-held grudges and learning new patterns of relating to others. This psychotherapy is most effective when it is combined with antidepressant medication, which can remedy chemical depletion in a person's brain that might otherwise hinder his or her ability to comprehend and respond to the counseling received."[3]

Physicians have noticed a correlation between physical illness and depression. Those that suffer from a heart attack or stroke, Parkinson's disease, and other hormonal disorders seem to be more likely to exhibit signs of depression. The recovery from an illness is often hindered by depression, and often the depression remains even after the physical ailment is resolved.

While researchers do not see a direct link between negative things happening in one's life and depression, certain environmental stresses may trigger the disorder. The death of a loved one, getting a divorce, or losing a job can elicit depression. Positive stresses such as moving, being promoted and having a baby can also potentially cause depression. As mentioned earlier, the way in which a person deals with stress may greatly affect his/her chances for developing depression.[4]

The Christmas of 1973 was the one of the worst times ever for me because, of course Christmas was always such a happy time and a time of year that I always looked forward to. Now the festivities the gift buying and giving the family get togethers were all just a means of intensifying my misery. It was just our third married Christmas together and I felt cheated and I felt like I was spoiling Barbara's holidays. All that I could do was fake it when I was around the family or friends and then collapse into a chair or the bed when I got home. I didn't know when or how I was ever gong to find my way out of this dark gloomy hole I was in. I remember telling Barbara that I really felt like I would have been a good father. I remember at that point I had no hope at all. I believed that our families would find out about my condition inevitably and I cringed at the thought. I was a total loser. Defective that's what I was! Some how I continued to go to work. I had to. No one knew that there was anything wrong with me except Barbara and my family doctor. Days seemed like they would never end. A day seemed like a week. To say that I was scared was an understatement. I knew that I was not right mentally; I didn't think of it as an emotional thing, I just thought that I was weak and defective. Whatever was the matter with me, I knew that it would be humiliating to me and even worse to Barbara, if people found out about it.

All things work to good for those who love the Lord and are called according to His purpose. Romans 8:28[5]

Again, I did not know this verse then, but now that I do, I can look back and see the truth in it, and I see God's hand in allowing it to happen. At least to my credit I didn't turn to illegal drugs or alcohol, I "gutted it out." I started running in the mornings before work, believing that if I made myself be more physically active it would relieve some of the numbing depression. My urologist encouraged me to exercise as well. I ran two miles every morning, and I wasn't eating very much because my appetite was gone. The result was that I went from about 180 lbs. to 159 lbs. I know I looked sickly. A few months after the holidays, I went to a psychologist who was absolutely no help. Eventually my family doctor suggested that I see a psychiatrist for my depression, and he told me further that my urethritis problem was a prostate problem and that I should also see a urologist. My family doctor put me on a very small dosage of lithium which did nothing for the depression, and didn't give me a whole lot of hope. I couldn't believe it. I considered myself a real man, I got through Viet-Nam, even survived an attempted assault on my position and here I was a depressed mess. My urologist, Dr. F.M. Price, had me x-rayed and discovered 2 large kidney stones, one that would require surgery and one that I might just barely pass if I built up enough pressure. He said that the kidney stones had caused an inflammation of the prostate, prostatitis or prostatosis. But he was almost as concerned about my emotional state as the surgery that I would have to undergo. He told me that exercise was good but that I had lost too much and I needed to change whatever I was doing. There was no lithotripsy back then; there was only slice and dice. He went on to be with the Lord in 1993, but he was as good a urologist as they come and so compassionate. Eventually I passed the smaller of the two kidney stones after drinking two or three beers one night strictly for that purpose and Dr. Price surgically removed the largest one in 1976. But those stones were the least of my concerns; I wanted to feel alive again instead of the life-numbing depression I was in.

I began to have panic attacks. A panic attack causes the fastest and most complex reaction known within the human body. The symptoms of panic attack include immediate alteration of the functioning of the eyes and major glands, the brain, the heart, lungs, stomach, intestines, pancreas, kidneys and bladder, and the major muscle groups. This physical response can lead to emotional responses such as belief that one is dying. Generally speaking, the more physical symptoms one has during an attack, the more emotionally devastating a panic attack can be. My panic attacks started when I would wonder if I were going to be trapped in this mental and emotional condition for the rest of my life. But later I would get panic attacks for bizarre things like getting paint somewhere that I didn't want while I was painting the house, or the brick patio that I built in the back not being perfect, silly things like that. Then I would get them at work, wondering if I designed something properly. As a civil engineer designing concrete and steel structures and evaluating existing structures, there is plenty to get panic attacks over if you are prone to get them. Sometimes I would come home and do structural calculations for hours while second-guessing myself. I would also imagine that I must have some kind of fatal disease and that I could be dying.

"There is another type of anxiety disorder called Generalized Anxiety Disorder (GAD). While it is normal to experience anxiety in reaction to dangerous, uncertain, or threatening situations, people with Generalized Anxiety Disorder experience anxiety constantly. People with GAD experience pathological anxiety which is excessive, chronic, and typically interferes with the ability to function normally in daily activities. Someone who suffers from GAD may worry about any and everything in his/her life.'[6]

CHAPTER 4

HOW DOES DEPRESSION MAKE YOU FEEL?

Harold Koenig, M.D. one of my favorite writers on the subject of depression related how one person felt in these terms: pain mixed with faith, drained and discouraged, helpless, empty, dejected, anxious, fearful, guilty, ashamed, needing to hide, exhausted, immersed in and smothered by darkness, weak, feeling like a failure, isolated and lonely, overwhelmed, stuck, confused, torn, desperate, immobilized, having lost a sense of normalcy. Having personally struggled with depression, I can identify with all of these feelings. In their book, "Depression, A Many Factored Thing", Dr. Koenig and David B. Biebel, D.Min. define depression thusly: *Depression is a state of existence marked by a sense of being pressed down, weighed down or burdened, which affects a person physically, mentally, spiritually and relationally. In other words, depression is not a state of mind but a state of being.*[1]

The psychiatrist was a kind man who listened patiently, as I poured out everything that I thought would help him. He said that based on what I had said; I needed to start taking anti-depressants and gradually workup to a maximum dose of 250 mg a night. My family doctor had prescribed the same medication but never more than 50 mg, thus it never worked. When I asked my psychiatrist how long it would take for the medication to make me feel normal again, he said four to six months. I was shocked and I told him that there was no way that I could go on feeling like this for six months. But then I reasoned to myself what choice did I have. The psychiatrist said that I should start feeling a little relief in two to three weeks. He explained that I had a chemical imbalance in my brain and that any stressful event could trigger the depressed state that I was in. Walking out of his office I wondered why me; why was the rug being jerked out from under me and my happy life. It had taken, after all, a long time to get to my happy life. At some point I began to pray. A hope did take root in my heart that I would experience joy again someday.

What is a chemical imbalance? A person's brain is a network of billions of nerve cells called neurons which communicate with one another to create cognitive (thought), affective (emotional) and behavioral responses. This process would not be possible without neurotransmitters, naturally occurring chemicals in the brain that are the key to cell-to-cell communication. Since this process is normally perfectly fine-tuned, any dysregulation may lead to changes in thinking, moods and your ability to function.

The term chemical imbalance or biological depletion is commonly used to define an irregularity that may exist in the production, absorption or reabsorption (reuptake) of neurotransmitters like Serotonin, Norepinephrine, Dopamine and GABA (Gamma-aminobutyric Acid). However, recent studies completed in the last decade indicate that the definition of a chemical imbalance should also encompass a variety of other natural chemicals, including vitamins, minerals, and amino acids which are essential to neurotransmitter synthesis. This is complicated stuff, bio-chemistry, and there are plenty of sources to find out more about it if you're interested. My research has shown that people who doubt the existence of chemical imbalances are misinformed at best and at worst are dangerous. They may be advising sufferers not to seek the help that they so desperately need.

The following depression statistics present a look at the scope of depression and how it affects adult men and women.

- Depression is a common emotional disorder affecting about 7% (13-14 million people) in any given year.

- Only 20% of those who experience depression will receive an appropriate treatment plan.
- 16% of all adults will experience depression.
- 97% of those suffering from depression say their work, home life, and relationships are negatively affected.
- Depression is the leading cause of disability in women.
- Depression in women usually occurs between the ages of 25 and 44.
- 7 million women in the United States are clinically depressed.
- 1 in 5 women will develop clinical depression over the course of her life.
- Only 1/3 of depressed women will seek professional help.
- About 19% of women will experience e post partum depression after childbirth.
- Women are twice as likely as men to develop depression.
- Though women experience depression twice as often as men, men are three times more likely to commit suicide.

- Suicide is most common among men who are separated widowed or divorced.
- Retired and unemployed men have a higher chance of developing depression.

According to the National Institute of Mental Health, chemical imbalances have been implicated in an array of emotional disturbances, like anxiety, panic attacks, depression and ADHD.[2]

Most of us will face a crisis in our lives, thrust at us without any kind of warning and without survival instructions. It has the potential to develop an unshakable faith that defies reality. A cup of sorrow can also be a cup of joy.

Chapter 5

Treatment

Depression can be treated and you can feel better again. I felt a great deal of comfort when I found that depression was a medical condition. Of course all sickness, death and disease came into the world because of the entrance of sin into the world through the fall of Adam. I had hope again. I was determined to get better. I had mixed reactions taking the medication, though. I'd been brought up not to turn to pills when I couldn't handle life's problems, and I didn't want to get hooked on them. I was ashamed that the problem was in my head. I wanted to rely on my own strength, not pills that might be hiding deeper problems. However I was desperate and I knew it. As scared as I was of the anti-depressants and their implication, I was even more scared of the darkness inside that was smothering me.

"The longer depression goes untreated, the harder it will be to treat effectively. Thankfully, we live in an era in which the downward spiral of depression can often be reversed through the cooperative effort of well-informed experts willing to confront what author Andrew Solomon called "the noonday demon" with an arsenal of medical, sociological and spiritual treatments. Such a multifaceted approach can facilitate the release of a depressed person from what seems like an inescapable dank, dark dungeon – one that only a generation ago was often endured in agonized silence."[1]

As a person who has benefited from these treatments, I see them as gifts from God that cannot in good conscience be withheld from those who need them on any basis-theological, philosophical, theoretical or otherwise.

The anti-depressants had a powerful effect on my brain. It wasn't a quick fix; in fact, there were times when I didn't think that it was helping. Sometimes I couldn't get words out immediately when I was speaking. But I began to have an occasional good day, and I realized that the medication was helping me to fight the depression and to deal head on with my problems no matter how painful it was. The medication was truly a miracle from God. If you find yourself feeling bad because you have to take anti-depressant medication because you feel like you ought to be depending on God, stop it. Who do you think puts healing power into any medication? Who would reject heart medication or antibiotics? I have never understood why people won't accept help when it's offered. Well I guess I understand, it's just so unfortunate. When God offers help, we need to take hold of it and be thankful, and swallow whatever pride is preventing us from doing so. If God's healing power were not in the medication, it would be like eating a capsule of dirt.

"Anyone who has been clinically depressed knows how hard it is to concentrate on anything, much less on understanding and applying biblical texts and principals to the practical issues of our lives. Taking medications so that your normal mental functions return, may actually pave the way for better understanding and application of God's truths to your life on a daily basis. Nor does taking medications imply that you are substituting a false god (medicine) and its truth for the real God and his truth. Medication in this case can facilitate deeper understanding of God's Word, a more cogent perception of faith, and a more coherent appropriation of the power of his Spirit. Those who hope in medicine will find only disappointment in the end; those who hope in God and use his medicine as a means to fulfilling his purposes quite often will find the healing they need.

Some Christian counselors may say that on medication you will be desensitized to God's Spirit, deaf to his voice. However, if you are clinically depressed you may never be able to discern God's voice until you find the right medication at the right dose to restore your equilibrium.'[2]

At some point after taking the medication for awhile I had a surprise happy moment, like the clouds opening up and a ray of light poking through the gloom. I hadn't had a feeling like that that in a very long time. It didn't last too long, but I began to have more and more of them and they lasted longer and longer. There were times when I felt that I had gone back to square one, but those times were getting fewer and farther between. Eventually I saw real progress, then some daylight until six months later; I was feeling better than I had in years, not a hint of depression or even anxiety. My chemicals were balanced! I bought the good psychiatrist a bottle of Jack Daniels Black and he said that I could start decreasing my dosage until I was back to none. I asked him if there was a chance that this could happen again. He said that if something happened to trigger the depression again, it could happen. But I couldn't imagine it, that's how stable I felt.

Every night I started thanking God for his mercy and for giving me my life back. That's how I felt, that God, in His mercy had literally found my life and given it back to me again. My relationship with God was still very shallow, however, still praying when I needed something and thanking Him when I received it. However, I did feel that God was merciful to me and cared about me. That was an immense improvement from the way I used to feel about Him. Barbara had a husband again, and I was so thankful. I was able to have fun with family and friends, enjoy my job, relax and take vacations again.

A few months later, however, I began to get obsessed with things and worry about my health. For example, anything that I did around the house, whether it be painting the exterior trim on the house or fixing a loose brick on the steps, it had to be perfect or I couldn't stop thinking about it. My ear would get stopped up and I would have to go to the doctor as soon as possible because I obsessed over it until it got fixed. Then there were the three or four kidney stones a year and the accompanying prostate trouble. Eventually I became depressed again to the point that I had to get with the psychiatrist and get back on anti-depressants. Another one to two month recovery time would ensue.

About this time Barbara became pregnant with Jared, and things were pretty sweet. I was a daddy, a life-changing event. In the depths of my depression I despaired over the fact that I was too messed up to be a father, but God had been merciful to me. Another subtle but life-changing event took place in our lives around this time, Barbara began attending a prayer group with some ladies and she realized that she needed something more in her life; and she knew that it was whatever they had in their lives. It was a personal relationship with Jesus Christ, and the knowledge that she was saved. I noticed the change in her one night as I was watching Monday Night Football. She would retreat to her bedroom and read the Bible. I too started reading the Bible but I couldn't understand it. I also wanted this personal relationship with Jesus Christ, but I didn't have a clue as to how to get it. I didn't know about it. All I knew was what the nuns and priests told us. I kept reading the Bible, and believed that it was God's Word; I just needed to understand it.

CHAPTER 6

GOD'S WORD

On March 30, 1980, in our bed, I gave my heart to the Lord, I asked Jesus to forgive me and to be my Lord and Savior. Tears of relief streamed down my face and I was reborn. Why it is that so many of us don't turn to God until we're at the end of our rope, I'll never know. I was saved and spiritually I felt fine, but my depression did not leave. I would read something in my Bible and the next day, I would think about it so intensely that an unreasonable fear would arise and I would erase the underlines that I made the previous day. Worry, fear and anxiety invaded every part of my life. All of it was completely irrational, but I could not control it. Somehow, I had to decide to let go of my unsuccessful control over this depression and hang on for dear life. I refused to relinquish something that I cherished. I cherished my life with Barbara, Jared and Joey.

Still I read the Bible even though I was afraid that I might read something that would upset me. I began to keep a journal and write down verses that I thought would help me. The first was Romans 12:2:

"And be not conformed to this world but be ye transformed by the renewing of your mind, that ye may prove what is that good, acceptable and perfect will of God"[1]

This was another life-changing event.

My mind definitely needed renewing. After several more severe bouts with depression, I saw a doctor who became our family physician, Dr. David Egleston. God surely sent me to him. He told me that what I had was very common, a chemical imbalance that causes clinical depression. Many people, he said, who are just like me lead normal lives by staying on an anti-depressant permanently, but not as large a dose as when you have been depressed for a long time. It was surprising that at this smaller dosage the side effects were relatively minor and was not harmful to the body. At the first visit we realized that we were both Christians. He explained to me that anti-depressants should be looked at as miracles provided to us by our Heavenly Father in His loving kindness.

And next I wrote down Philippians 2:13:

"For it is God who worketh in you both to will and to do of His good purpose"[2]

The King James is beautiful, but I sometimes had difficulty grasping some of it so I bought myself a Parallel version with the King James Version on one side of the page and the Living Version on the other side. The Living Version is written in the way that we speak today and it really helped me. In Corinthians 5:17-18, I found that I was a new creation and that the old creation is gone. The old Virgil was gone. I liked that. That was exciting to know, but I didn't know what miracles would result for me later from that scripture. The same was true for Mark 11:24, where Jesus said:

"I tell you therefore; everything you ask and pray for, believe that you have it already, and it will be yours"[3]

This verse would have a profound effect on my life, and help with the healing that I desperately needed. Keep in mind that my chemical imbalance was still crippling if I weren't on anti-depressants. I felt such emotional pain that I can't describe it except to say that I would much rather endure physical pain.

Other verses from the Bible that I wrote in my journal were, 1 Corinthians 15:51, 52, Psalms 19:14, James 3:13, 1 John 1: 4 and Matthew 7:7-11. I'll let you look these up. Matthew 7:7-11 is a scripture that is typed in red in my Bible. That means that Jesus said it. His words are always true.

"Ask and it shall be given you; seek and ye shall find; knock, and it shall be opened unto you:

For everyone that asketh receiveth; and he that seeketh findeth; and to him that knocketh it shall be opened."

Or what man is there of you, whom if his son ask bread, will he give him a stone? Or if he ask a fish, will he give him a serpent? If ye then being evil know how to give good gifts unto your children, how much more shall your Father which is in heaven give good things to them that ask Him?"[4]

Matthew 7:7-11 became the scripture that I always turned to when I was having problems. All of Jesus' words are Living Water to me, but Matthew 7:7-11 was spoken especially for me and countless other souls I'm sure.

Sometimes I wonder why me! Or why couldn't there have been any other way to get it! God told me that it was the only way for me. He allowed me to go through it. I was a weak imperfect person who thought that he was a pretty good guy. God offers us strength, strength that is somehow perfected in weakness (2 Corinthians 12:9)[5]. On an ordinary day we may feel like we can make it just fine without God and His Word, but raise the stress to a certain level and we realize that our strength isn't coming from us. He offers us peace, "peace that passeth every thought". (Philippians 4:7)[6]

"The Bible is the one book to which every

thoughtful man may go to with any honest question of life or destiny and find the answer of God by honest searching" – John Ruskin

Other scriptures that I wrote down about this time in my little spiral notebook were Psalm 112:1-4, Deuteronomy 6: 4-9, Isaiah 3:10, Jeremiah 17:7,8, John 7:38, Acts 1:11, John 14:3 and Romans 10: 9,10.

God is not concerned with our legal obsessions but with our being new creations. Scriptural references for this are: Galatians 6:15, Galatians 5: 4, Corinthians 5:17, Romans 7:6, and Colossians 2:8. The reality of being able to become a new creation was totally foreign to me and I didn't understand it at all, nor did I foresee the enormous impact on my life that this transformation would bring.

Getting through life one day at a time, and searching the Word of God was my daily routine. I was praying daily to God to help me be a good husband and a father. By this time I had two young boys, Jared and Joey and Barbara was sticking with me and all of us were growing spiritually. Barbara really needed God because life with me was pretty chaotic. We attended a Bible study once a week and we learned a lot there. One interesting entry that I made in my notebook was, "Yield completely to Jesus and put your growing into His hands. Trust Him with it absolutely and always. Accept whatever comes to you each moment as being the sunshine or rain needed for that moment's growth". Scriptural references were Philippians 4:6, Psalm 92:12-14, John 15:1-5, Joel 2:22, 25, 26, Hosea 14:4-7, Jeremiah 17: 7,8 and Isaiah 35:1 and 35:7.

A thought that I wrote down which I wish I could have learned earlier, but with a chemical imbalance it's not easy: "At the end of any action never indulge in any reflection of any kind; whether self-congratulatory or despair. Forget the things that are behind you the moment they are past and leave them with God."

The thought of being a new creation must have really intrigued me at this time because I wrote: "It does not matter if a person is circumcised or not; what matters is for him to become an altogether new creature. Peace and mercy to all who follow this rule, who form the Israel of god."[7]

Galatians 6: 15

"But now we know we are rid of the Law, freed by death from our imprisonment, free to serve in the new spiritual way and not the old way of a written law."[8]

Romans 7:6

Around 1983 I began to see that a lot of things I used to believe were in error, like belonging to the right church would get you into heaven. But I wrote in my journal: "…because it's God's Kingdom that counts, not man's kingdom. God wants to bring life to the churches; He doesn't read the names over the churches."

Painfully I had learned that maturity is never instant; but I learned that revelation can be. What do I mean when I say revelation? By that I mean that God just shows me something in an instant. He just pops it right in my head. It's usually a truth from the Bible but it could be about anything. That reminds me that one thing I will always be glad about was that we taught our kids, Jared and Joey about God before they even knew what we were talking about practically. Barbara and I wanted to be certain that whenever the light bulb came on and they started learning and understanding they would be hearing and learning about God as well. Read Deuteronomy 6.

Right before I had my last meltdown, I'll call it, I wrote in my journal: (God knew what I was going to encounter). Trust the Lord that you will be purified when you come out of this furnace.

God's Word will always reveals something new to you that you never noticed before, no matter how many times you have read it. For example the Psalms:

"God has given sacred promises, no wonder I exult."[9]

Psalm 108:7

"He gives food to those who trust Him; He never forgets His promises." [10]

Psalm 111:5

"Praise the Lord! For all who fear God and trust in Him are blessed beyond expression." [11]

Psalm 112:1

"Now spare me by your kindness and by your love. Then I will have an answer for those who taunt me." [12]

Psalm 119:42

"May I never forget your Words, for they are my only hope." [13]

Psalm 119:43

"All those who fear and trust in Him will welcome me because I too am trusting in Your Word."[14]

Psalm 119:74

"Forever, O Lord, Your Word stands firm in heaven" [15]

Psalm 119:89

"Nothing is perfect except Your Word" [16]

Psalm 119:96

"I have refused to walk the path of evil for I will remain obedient to Your Word" [17]

Psalm 119:101

"I am close to death at the hands of my enemies; oh give me my life back again." [18]

Psalm 119:107

"Early in the morning before the sun is up, I am praying and pointing out how much I trust in You. I stay awake through the night to think about Your promises." [19]

Psalm 119:147

It's easy to see that God's promises are a part of my everyday life and I love to read about them in the Bible. His Words are perfect and they stand forever. They are my answer to those who taunt me, namely Satan. God has given His promises and He never forgets them.

People who have real faith are certain of one thing among others – that God will keep His Word. "They are certain that what we do not see – His very existence and the realm of the eternal – is more real than anything that can be seen with purely human eyes or imagined with the human mind. "[20]

CHAPTER 7

OBSESSIVE THOUGHTS

I became obsessed about my prostate problem thinking that it was my fault, because of a pamphlet on prostate problems from the doctor's office and concluded that I had some strange germs that I could not get rid of. The doctor told me that was not what it meant, but Satan used these thoughts to cripple me, hurt me and rob me of my Joy. This obsession plagued me for about three years.

While I was almost over this neurosis, Satan attacked me from a different angle. Perfection became a daily necessity. Everything that I did had to be absolutely perfect, whether it was painting the house, fixing a loose brick on the steps or trying to have a perfect lawn. From no one else did I demand perfection, but for me it was, "Do it perfectly or don't do it." There were some times that I was not on an anti-depressant and I really struggled chemically. This was before I got on medication on a continual basis instead of "as needed". Satan attacked me in other areas of my life. Cautiously, I was getting past my anxiety over physical problems and perfectionist ways. Satan knew that since I had become born again and reading the Bible daily, the best way to strike at me was to twist God's Word and use it against me.

I read in the Bible that blasphemy against the Holy Ghost was an unforgivable sin. During my Catholic upbringing, this had been a great fear for me that I might take communion with a sin on my soul and this was called a sacrilege. I remember being terrified of committing a sin that was "too bad for God to forgive". If I had remained a Catholic this awful fear, I believe would have triggered a depression. Satan brought that fear back with a vengeance as I struggled with depression. Now as bizarre as this is going to sound, I'm going to tell you what happened to me around 1983. Barbara and I had the kids at Chuck E. Cheese and we were having a great time. We were watching one of our kids playing a game and he was getting a huge score. I went to say "Holy Smokes", but what came out was "Holy Ghost". I was shocked and thought, "Where did that come from?" It was a total accident. But the more I thought about it and fretted about it, the more of a problem it became. The difference between true guilt and false guilt was irrelevant to me as it is to most depressed people. My perception was so warped by depression that I consistently adopted the most negative interpretation possible of events or conversations.

Impaired memory and thinking is a devastating consequence of depression. The scripture kept coming back to me and I now know that Satan was using it against me. I was constantly replaying the incident in my mind and my imagination began to run wild. I thought all kinds of bizarre thoughts. A huge downward spiral was underway. I believe that I knew Satan was behind this even back then but I panicked and became depressed. The enemy caused me to be concerned about my salvation. Satan is the ultimate bully and attacks us at our weakest points; he wants to defeat us so that we will not be effective for God. As I obsessed over this, Satan began to put the foulest words in my mind linked to the precious name of Jesus, and the harder I tried to put them out of my mind, the harder they stuck.

Still God loved me and had mercy on me. He kept me going and I kept reading His Word. Going through the Book of Proverbs I came across a particular string of verses where Solomon was particularly harsh concerning a particular sin. Guess what? Another serious concern about my salvation resulted over this. Was Satan trying to make me gun-shy over reading the Bible? In hindsight, yes, but I didn't see that then. All scripture is profitable for teaching or correction and certain portions of the Old Testament, Proverbs for example, contain concepts or teachings that are obviously general principals for guidance in faith (most likely aimed at teaching these principals to the young).

I imagined that God had deserted me and was punishing me for my failures. I could not achieve the perfection that I so desperately sought for and this thinking, together with my chemical imbalance and inability to see the positive, got the best of me for a long time. I was seriously messed up concerning God and His Word and yet I knew that God and His Word were my only hope. I didn't know how or what to pray for, I just knew that I needed a miracle. God knew that and gave me a miracle in the way of a dream.

In the dream, Barbara, Jared Joey and I were in our car parked near a wooded area. Suddenly there was a snake in our car, in my lap I think; and it kept trying to bite me. I yelled at Barbara and the boys to get out of the car. Then I got out of the car. I got back into the car, grabbed the snake, and flung it into the woods.

The interpretation: You will struggle with the devil, Satan, but you will defeat him. That is the first and only time I have ever had a dream and an interpretation to it. This event was really a turning point for me, knowing that God was communicating with me. I wrote the following entries in my journal:

God's Word is Truth and final.

You will be with me in Paradise.

You know that all of these Good Words come from God

Because the devil would never tell you anything good for fear That you might do some good because of it.

My child know that all your sins are forgiven. I love you.

Love Me. Love and devote yourself to your family.

Love your neighbors.

The devil has told you many lies in the past. I will make those lies and the memories of those lies as though they were not.

Bad thoughts come from the devil and bring worry. Good thoughts

Come from the Holy Spirit and bring peace.

All depression, fear, worry, anxiety and doubt come from the devil.

God is all merciful, all loving and that's why He sent His Son Jesus to die for our sins.

The fact that Jesus had a personal interest in me helped me get a spiritual perspective on everything. Looking through the scriptures I would find ones that related to me and write them down.

John 16:23 "Whatsoever ye ask the Father in My Name, He will give it to you"[1] I asked God for forgiveness of all my sins in Jesus' Name, so I know they are all forgiven.

John 14:26 "But the Comforter, Who is the Holy Spirit Whom the Father will send in My Name, He shall teach ye all things and bring all things to your remembrance, whatsoever I have said unto you"[2]

I asked for the Holy Spirit in Jesus' name so I know that I have the Holy Spirit and He speaks to me.

John 3:16 "*...So that anyone who believes in Me will have eternal life. For God loved the world so much that He gave His only Son so that anyone who believes in Him shall not perish but have eternal life."*[3]

John 14:4 "Yes, ask anything using my name and I will do it"[4]

How wonderful and simple these words are, a child can understand it, and I was relying on God's Word more and more.

God told me that I was a special child of His and to lay my burdens down at the foot of the cross. This may seem like a small thing, but the Holy

Spirit told me not to worry and that he helps me in all areas, but he helps me the most in the areas that I needed help the most. I really needed to hear that.

It is better for a man to do a small task well than to do a large task poorly.

God confirmed the fact that my chemical imbalance was the cause of my depression, and that he will heal it. He wanted me to be a confident Christian. He told me that I was a Christian man.

He told me something else pretty awesome and he tells me this repeatedly "Your sins are like they never happened. He said that my body had been cleaned as perfectly as my soul. Nothing goes in there and stays permanently." He told me further that Christians can call their mistakes learning experiences.

We are not bound by the Old Testament. No one could enter heaven until Jesus died for our sins, and a New Covenant was made between God and man and it is, "that all manner of sin shall be forgiven unto man." Jesus said that He would send another Comforter and that He will never leave you. He is the Holy Spirit Who leads to all Truth. (See John 14)

Acts 10:43 "And the prophets have written about Him, saying that everyone who believes in Him will have their sins forgiven through His

Name."[5]

Luke 7:45 "A good man produces good deeds from a good heart."[6]

Elsewhere in the Bible, Jesus says, "Do you know what you are saying when you call Me good, because only God is truly good."[7]

I think in Luke 7:45, Jesus was saying that a good man has God in him and that's why he does good deeds from a good heart."

Always remember…Jesus said it, I believe it and that settles it.

I was a big time worrier. I think a lot of that was the chemical imbalance, not all of it because a lot of it was from spiritual immaturity. I guess I was just insecure about life in general. I didn't have a spiritual foundation, what I had was a fear of God and always scared of sinning. My imagination would run wild at times and I would question my salvation. I spoke of some specific instances of that earlier. I was assured of my salvation, but in my condition doubts plagued me. I became obsessed with reassuring myself that I was saved and that God did love me and cared about me. I was so scared of how weak my faith was. I read the gospels over and over clinging to one scripture after another. *Philippians 4:6 says, "Don't worry about anything but instead pray about everything."*[8] That's one of the first verses I memorized. The Holy Spirit told me one time, “Don’t worry about worrying.” That’s how bad off I was.

I once heard that if you’re having a really bad time or struggle, spiritually, that’s because you are running head on into the devil; and to do that you have to be running in the opposite direction from him…and that’s good. It makes sense.

A scripture that became dear to my heart was Luke 21:33:

“Heaven and Earth will pass away, but my words shall not pass away.”[9]

That verse was important because the words that Jesus spoke were the only thing that kept me going. They were the anchor for my soul and my entire being. And no one can take them away from me.

CHAPTER 8

A DEFINING MOMENT

I had two defining moments in my life, the first was when I was saved; the other came a few years after I was saved. It was sometime in the early 80's. I decide that I had to either believe God's Word or not; and I decided that I would. No matter what the circumstances were in my life or were to come; I would take God at His Word. That was my second defining moment.

That second defining moment had nothing to do with what denomination I belonged to, or if I had raised my hand at a service. "Faith's issue today as always, is: Are you willing to keep walking with God despite the adversity He may allow you to experience, because you trust that in everything He allows, He is motivated by love and acting with your good in mind? If your answer is 'yes' and you actually fulfill it (although maybe not perfectly), others will notice it and demand to know the reason for the hope that is in you."[1] (See 1 Peter 3:15)[2]

Clinical depression cannot just be willed away, as much as we would like to think that it can.

It's too insidious, too cruel for that. It does no good to fight it except in the sense that we will not let it win. We must instead give in. The time must come for us to admit to ourselves that we need help in whatever form God has made available. I have known too many men and women that for whatever reason chose to bear the unbearable load and finally succumb; and I have known even more that desperately wanted to live and escape the horror and pain. Innumerable situations of pain are bearable because one knows that there will be relief eventually, there will be the sweetness of normalcy once again when they are reunited with their loved ones again, pain-free. Even during the period of pain there is a sense of understanding and acceptance, because of the knowledge of the cause of the invasion into one's life. Not so for the sufferer of clinical depression, who does not know where the invasion came from and more frightful, where it is going. There is no hope for tomorrow; there are no joyous plans for a joyful reunion with loved ones. There is never any relief from the mind-numbing despair. Every human experience that normally gives joy, peace and happiness only adds to the pain of the clinically depressed. For those afflicted, their life goes on but it seems to be a suspended life quite different than life that continues all around them.

But in spite of this dismal picture that I have painted, a picture of myself 32 years ago, sweet reunion to life is near to all that are trapped in this gray fog where light cannot be seen.

It begins with a moment where your surrender, and decide that you are going to do everything that is medically and spiritually necessary to return to life that was once embraceable. I had gotten to the point where the only slight relief came in the late afternoon when I returned to the familiar surroundings of my home, in a controlled environment to some degree. Nothing was required of me after the sun set and I could just sit in a chair and turn on the television. Barbara was completely unaware of the severity of my situation. She knew I was down, but like in many cases, even the spouse cannot read another's mind or feel their pain. It isn't as though one can describe what they are feeling, because it is utterly indescribable. I know that I have done a woefully inadequate job at my attempt to do it.

How do you think God feels about our plight? We know from the attitude of Jesus who was gentle, merciful and kind toward those who are suffering.

"...a bruised reed He will not break, and a smoldering wick He will not snuff out"[3]

Matthew 12:20

He will leave the ninety-nine that is tucked safely in the fold and find and rescue the one who is lost.

Life is too precious a gift not to take advantage of all that the Lord has to offer us and retrieve it. A moment came for me when I realized that I would swallow my pride, not that I had any left, and be responsible enough to admit that I had a serious problem. That decision put me on a path that would not only restore my physical and mental health, but put me on the much narrower path that led me to my Savior and my salvation. I may never have found this path had it not been for the terrifying dimensions of the predicament that came upon me that fall some thirty-two years ago. I know Jesus was there over thirty-one years ago urging me on, picking me up when I was at my weakest and darkest moment. I didn't know it then, I was just trying to survive with a tiny flicker of hope that I could be restored, although I didn't have any idea of how or how long it would take.

After restoration some six months later, and the subsequent relapses that occurred in my case, I knew that I needed more help and found myself needing to get back on the medication.

CHAPTER 9

FORGIVE YOURSELF

If you are someone that cannot forgive himself/herself, when the Lord forgives your sins He forgets them. He makes them not as though they were. He throws them into the sea of forgetfulness. You should forget your sins after you have asked forgiveness because they are gone. Why remember something or worry about something that doesn't exist. That's like worrying about Attila the Hun.

While you are growing and recovering from depression, remember that some mysteries you will not fully understand until you get to heaven; but the Holy Spirit will always give you understanding of the verses that you really need to understand.

Do you realize that when you believe in God's Words you are a new creation? The Holy Spirit told me that. The Holy Spirit comforted me once by telling me not to be concerned by the feeling of depression, it's just a feeling. This was a time in my life when I wasn't depressed about anything in particular, I was just totally depressed. I couldn't smile. It was obviously totally chemical. I was so vulnerable in that time of my life.

But I wrote in my journal, "Another thought was of God's two hands stretched out toward me and then holding me, which is a sign that God loves me". I continued to write, "Another thought was of me sitting at the feet of God, which shows how much I love Him". (See how important it is to keep a journal? I would never have remembered all of these things.)

Continuing to be unsure of my salvation, struggling daily, God's Word and the Holy Spirit were my only comfort. Acts 10:43…

"And the prophets have written about Him, saying that anyone who believes in Him will have their sins forgiven through His Name."[1]

"He that believeth on Him is not condemned." John 3:18[2]

I wrote, "I believe in Him and on Him" (wanting to get it right.)

"As the scriptures express it,' See, I am sending Christ to be the carefully chosen, precious Cornerstone of My church and I will never disappoint those who trust in Him" 1 Peter 2:6[3]

These were scriptures that helped me make it through another day. The Holy Spirit told me that nervousness comes from the enemy. This was at a time when I was trying to make it on my own without medication. I began having a guilt complex.

For a time when I was pursuing my hobby of digging and collecting old bottles, there were occasions when permission had not been given to dig. I began to panic and wonder how I could make this situation right. I even took some bottles and placed them on top of a concrete block wall adjacent to where we dug once, but there was no way to remember all of the places that I dug and what I found. The Holy Spirit told me that when I was saved I was forgiven for my sins. There was no further action required and the sins were as though they were never committed. I was so sorry, and yet there was nothing that I could do to make it right. I was forced to rest in God's peace and forgiveness. It felt wonderful.

"All scripture is given by inspiration of God and is profitable for doctrine, for reproof, for correction and for instruction in righteousness."[4]

2 Timothy 3:16

"I acknowledge my sins unto thee, and mine iniquity have I not hid. I said I will confess my transgressions unto the Lord; and then forgive me the iniquity of my sin."[5]

Psalm 32:5

"Your Heavenly Father will forgive you if you forgive those who sin against you; but if you

refuse to forgive them, He will not forgive you."[6]

Matthew 6:14, 15

"And we know that all that happens to us is working for our good if we love God and are fitting into His plans."[7]

Romans 8:28

"Seek ye first the Kingdom of God...[8]

"Trust in the Lord with all your heart; and lean not on thine own understanding."

Proverbs 3:5

"He that hath the Son, hath life."[9]

1 John 5:12

"I come that they might have life and that they might have it more abundantly."[10]

John 10:10

If you are comforted by a thought, it is from the Holy Spirit. God lives in me in the form of the Holy Spirit. John 14:15-18 shows that the Father, Son and Holy Spirit lives within us. And the closeness of God is further emphasized in John 14:20, *"At that day ye shall know that I am in My Father, and ye in me and I in you."*[11]

The Holy Spirit told me to be content to know

that you are in God's will, and serve Him and your family.

The enemy will never give you a comforting thought, therefore any thought that gives you comfort comes from The Comforter. This was at least the second time that the Holy Spirit told me this. It was for emphasis. Throughout the last 25 years or so many, many messages and scriptures were repeated for emphasis.

CHAPTER 10

WHO SUFFERS WITH DEPRESSION?

Stan's Story

Depression–a word that is used frequently in our time. Does it apply to you, someone you love, or someone you know? Since 17 percent of the population suffers from major depression at some point in their lives, [1] it is probable you have been touched by it in some way. Perhaps the following account will "ring true" in light of your experiences. (This story really happened, but the name of the character has been changed.)

For many years Stan, an evangelical Christian, struggled with varying degrees of depression. These bouts were incapacitating on occasion, irritating or highly frustrating sometimes, but always persistent in their visits. Eventually the struggle came to a crisis point. He was not able to respond to any emotional stimulus that was offered; he had totally isolated himself from family, friends, and work. In retrospect he realized this isolation was done purposefully. The true causes of his struggle had never been addressed, and he was tired of pulling himself out of one depressed state only to find another staring him in the face. So he refused to repeat the pattern that had plagued him for so many years. It was time to find the root causes, instead of repeatedly dodging them. After talking with a good friend who was a counselor, he decided he should consider admitting himself to a psychiatric hospital. He immediately contacted such a place and entered the "first phase," or initial analysis prior to admittance. This analysis indicated he should become a patient. The next day he became part of an extraordinary program of discovery that was to last more than three weeks. In fact, those weeks were so extraordinary; he will tell you they provided the impetus for dramatic, positive change in his life and thought.

During those days of concentration, Stan dealt with several important issues that subsequently have led to a more stable life. First, he faced the trauma of abuse he had experienced. Second, through the ministry of a compassionate chaplain and a counselor, he realized he was weary of learning about God, without at the same time knowing God in the personal way the Bible frequently indicates. He was hungry to couple Biblical precepts with personal experience. Third, the sense of community among those in the hospital with him led him to consider the social "games" he had been playing in his evangelical Christian setting outside the hospital. Even though many of the patients were not Christians, that did not deter them from intimacy, trust, and truth. There were no hidden agendas, no political posturing, and no hypocritical fronts. They listened to one another, cried together, encouraged one another, challenged one another, laughed together, and even disciplined one another. Fourth, Stan was challenged to consider whether he should take medication in light of his trust in God's healing power. He was put on medication that is still part of his life after eight years. Fifth, he was led to consider his thought life, especially as it applied to expectations he had of himself.

Unfortunately, there are many Christians who continue to wrestle with what Winston Churchill called the "black dog" of depression. They struggle without finding help. This essay is offered with the hope that it will encourage those who need help, and that it will prompt many to respond with patience and love to those who are depressed.

Who Suffers with Depression?

Some have said depression is "the common cold of emotional disorders, and it appears to be on the rise. People of both genders get depressed, although women are twice as likely as men to suffer from major depressive disorders."[2] Who are these people? As we will see, they are both famous and infamous people; they are normal people; they are even people we know from the Bible. Depression can be described as "a condition of general emotional dejection and withdrawal; sadness greater and more prolonged than that warranted by any objective reason."[3] Dejection, withdrawal, sadness, and other similar terms are familiar to many. Vincent Van Gogh, Abraham Lincoln, Edgar Allen Poe, Marilyn Monroe, Rod Steiger, Mike Wallace, and many other notable people have struggled with depression.

In 1972 Senator Thomas Eagleton acknowledged his depression, and the Democrats dropped him as the Vice Presidential candidate. In 1995 Alma Powell, the wife of General Colin Powell, revealed her history of depression, and her husband urged others to get help.[4] Martin Luther and Charles Spurgeon, two great men in the history of the church, frequently lived with the dark shadow of despondency. Even some great biblical characters wrestled with depression. At one point in his life, Moses wanted to die (Exodus 32:32). While struggling with his suffering, Job "cursed the day of his birth" (3:1). He said, "I will speak in the anguish of my spirit, I will complain in the bitterness of my soul" (7:11). In addition, he cried, "My spirit is broken, my days are extinguished, the grave is ready for me" (17:1).

At one point, Lincoln wrote: "I am now the most miserable man living. If what I feel were distributed equally to the whole human family, there would not be one cheerful face on earth. Whether I shall ever be better, I cannot tell. I awfully forbode that I shall not. To remain as I am is impossible, I must die or be better, it appears to me."

During this bout with depression, friends kept knives and razors away from Lincoln, and he did not carry a pocketknife for months.

Elijah was incapacitated with depression soon after he had been an integral player in one of the great demonstrations of God's power (I Kings 19). After Jonah witnessed the astounding grace of God among the wicked Ninevites, he angrily said, "Death is better to me than life" (Jonah 4:3). The great prophet Jeremiah declared, "Why did I ever come forth from the womb to look on trouble and sorrow?" (Jeremiah 20:18) The amazing prophecy of Isaiah 53:3 states that the Suffering Servant, the Lord Jesus, was "a man of sorrows, and acquainted with grief."

Sorrows and grief can refer to both physical and mental pain, which could include depression.[5]

Consider the thoughts of Lydia Child, the 19th century abolitionist, in light of Isaiah 53:

Whatever is highest and holiest is tinged with melancholy. The eye of genius has always a plaintive expression, and its natural language is pathos. A prophet is sadder than other men; and He who was greater than all the prophets was "a man of sorrows and acquainted with grief."[6] A well-known spiritual says, "No one knows the trouble I've seen," a sentiment that is understood by those who are depressed. J.B. Phillips, author of the classic, *Your God is Too Small*, dealt with depression all his life. In one of his many letters, he offered these comments to one who also was struggling: "As far as you can, and God knows how difficult this is, try to relax in and upon Him. As far as my experience goes, to get even a breath of God's peace in the midst of pain is infinitely worth having."[7] We have seen that depression has been experienced since ancient times. No one is immune, but, praise God, those in His family are not alone. The Lord Himself is with us.

Depression: Symptoms and Explanations

I feel so tired!

I feel weak; my arms are heavy.

I feel so agitated!

I feel anxious about everything, it seems.

I feel so fearful–of death, of tomorrow, of people.

I can't concentrate!

I can't remember things I used to remember.

I can't face people; I want to be alone.

I'm not interested in sex anymore.

I can't sleep!

I sleep to escape!

I only eat because I have to.[8]

I hate myself!

I feel angry all the time!

Everything and everyone is stupid!

Such comments are familiar to those who are dealing with depression. Usually these phrases are not descriptive of what is objectively true, but they are descriptive of how a depressed person is responding to his predicament. One who hears them can be tempted to dismiss the one who made the statements with well-meaning but trite responses that betray a lack of understanding. It often is difficult for someone who has not wrestled with depression to understand. So how can we understand? Why does a person get depressed? There is no simple answer to this question, contrary to what some people think. As Dr. John White has written, "Depression has many faces. It cannot be relieved on the basis of one simple formula, arising as it does by numerous and complex mechanisms, and plummeting sometimes to depths where its victims are beyond the reach of verbal communication. There are mysteries about it which remain unsolved. No one theoretical framework is adequate to describe it."[9] It is meaningful for a Christian to understand this. Sometimes a response to the depressed can focus on a principle without regard for the person. For example, the 17th century English bishop Jeremy Taylor wrote: "It is impossible for that man to despair who remembers that his Helper is omnipotent."[10] This assumes that remembering something will automatically change one's thoughts and feelings. The person who is depressed doesn't necessarily make that connection. Mentally healthy people have reasonable thought processes, but they are not the norm in a depressed person's clouded life. "Mental health is like physical health. We are all vulnerable to its loss."[11] A truly depressed person is not mentally healthy. As we have stated, there is no one all-encompassing answer to the "Why?" of depression. But there are a number of models that suggest answers.

Aggression turned inward or unexpressed anger.

Object loss, as in the loss of a parent.

Loss of self-esteem.

Incorrect thinking.

Learned helplessness, or inability to respond to unpleasant experiences. Loss of reinforcement, as in lack of sympathy.

Loss of role status, as in loss of power or prestige.

Loss of meaning of existence.

Impairment of brain chemistry, as in neurotransmitters.

Neurophysiological malfunction of brain cells. [12]

When we ponder these models in the light of a Christian worldview, we find that none of them can stand alone. Each one taken separately reduces us to only one element, whereas a Christian worldview sees man holistically. Man is not to be seen solely as a product of his past, his thought life, his societal conditioning, or his biology. The one who is depressed should be approached as Christ would: as a whole person made in God's image.

Depression and the Whole Person

"What is man that you are mindful of him, the son of man that you care for him?" These memorable phrases from Psalm 8 pose crucial questions in regard to the subject of depression. The answers we give to such questions will provide a beginning point for responding to those who are depressed. As Leslie Stevenson has written, "The prescription for a problem depends on the diagnosis of the basic cause."[13] A Christian is challenged to consider a prescription for depression that sees both the material and immaterial aspects of a total person. Such considerations lead to concerns as to whether one should take medication, submit to some type of psychological analysis, or simply trust God to provide healing. Or, as a prominent Christian psychiatrist asks, "Is [depression] a disease of the mind or of the body?"[14] Is it both/and, or either/or? These are issues that tend to stir controversy among Christians. Too frequently the controversy is focused on "clumsy clichés ...subtly damning exhortations, breezy banalities, and the latest idiocy in pop psychology. Or else...unnecessary pills."[15]

The history of the church demonstrates that one of the reasons for such a response is found in an ancient struggle between Greek and Hebrew influences. More often than not we tend to side with the Greeks and divide humans "into a less important physical part (body and brain) and a more important immaterial part (mind and soul)."[16] This unbiblical division creates problems, because "just as music is more than the orchestra that plays it, so I am more than my body."[17] I am also more than my mind and soul. When this unity of human nature is ignored two extreme views can be found among Christians. "One is that we submit to all suffering, sickness, pain—whether mental or physical–as from God."[18] The other asserts that "through the exercise of faith and by the power of Jesus' name we can banish every sickness, every difficulty. Sickness, tragedy, pain must be resisted, for all come from Satan. Unhappiness is a sign of defeat and unbelief."[19] This means that seeking help from physicians, psychologists, or psychiatrists "is a tacit admission that the resources in Christ and the Scripture are inadequate."[20] Both of these views are too simplistic, but there are certainly elements of the truth in them. How can we reconcile them?

Quite simply and obviously, the one who is depressed should be treated as a whole person.

Consider the statements of John White, a practicing Christian psychiatrist, author of a thought-provoking book on depression and suicide entitled *The Masks of Melancholy*, and many other books. He wrote:

I will no more treat mind as distinct from body than body as distinct from mind. By the grace of God I will treat persons, not pathology, sinners rather than syndromes, and individuals rather than illnesses. And however primitive our weapons may be, there are effective weapons and we must use them.[21]

As one who has fought with depression, I

have come to realize the wisdom of Dr. White's comments. The treatment I have received has come from family, friends, physicians, psychologists, and psychiatrists who understand how God has created us. Their compassionate, godly responses to my struggle have been instrumental in my recovery. To paraphrase the apostle Paul, "I thank my God in all my remembrance of [them]" (Philippians 1:3). They were the Lord's servants in my time of need.

Responding to Depression.

Sarah's husband has been isolating himself from her for several weeks. He won't communicate with her. He doesn't eat much. He shows no emotion other than a sense of sadness and gloom. He sits in the dark for hours. He has called his office several days to report he is taking a sick day. He does none of the things he once did that gave him a sense of joy and accomplishment. He shows no interest in making love with her. He has disappeared for hours in his car and will not say where he has been. Sarah wonders if she has done something to upset him and is desperate to get him to talk with her so she can discover what is happening.

Perhaps this scenario is familiar to you or someone you know. How can we respond to such a crisis? How can we help the one who is depressed?

First, understand the difference between

someone who is sad or disheartened and someone who is truly depressed. Sadness or a "blue mood" are experienced by most of us. Depression is much more debilitating and long-lasting. There are at least three levels of depression. One can be called major depression, which "is manifested by a combination of symptoms that interfere with the ability to work, sleep, eat, and enjoy once pleasurable activities." Another, called dysthymia, is less severe but keeps one "from functioning at `full steam' or from feeling good." The third level is called manic-depressive, or bipolar depression. This "involves cycles of depression and elation or mania."[22]

Second, if you believe someone is struggling continually with depression, encourage him or her to seek help. Suggest that your friend see a trusted pastor, counselor, or physician. The earlier you can suggest this, the better.

Third, at the first sign of depression, encourage conversation and then listen carefully. The deeper a person sinks into a depressed state, the more difficult it is to talk with anyone, even those they love most. Make yourself available and gently pursue communication as often as you can. But leave time for silence when you are with them.

Fourth, give emotional support that indicates you are taking the person seriously. "Do not accuse the depressed person of faking illness or of laziness, or expect him or her `to snap out of it'."[23]

Fifth, be an encourager. Affirm the one who is depressed with statements of truth about his character and abilities, as well as your love for him.

Sixth, if they will let you, pray for them in their presence.

Seventh, if you hear remarks about suicide, take them seriously and seek advice from an expert.

Eighth, act as a "mental mirror." They probably aren't thinking reasonably and are in need of gentle reminders of a clearer image of the world and themselves.

Ninth, don't chastise them if they express anger, even anger at God. Listen carefully to discover why they are angry and help them begin to think how they can best express that anger.

Tenth, on a larger scale, do what you can to develop an atmosphere in your church that allows one who is depressed to find trust, truth, and compassion. These ten suggestions, as helpful as they can be, do not constitute the ultimate response to the depressed. We need to remember that ultimate healing rests in the hands of our loving God, who makes all things new.

There is some debate as to whether antidepressant medication is addictive, and whether it could cause suicidal thoughts. I strongly suggest you discuss this issue with your doctor, as they should have up-to-date information.

If you go to a doctor and ask for treatment for depression, it's possible that you will be given antidepressant medication. Medication can help a lot of people who are depressed, in combination with some form of therapy.

As with any medication, you should follow the advice of your doctor closely about dosage, length of time to be taking the pills, drug interactions, things to avoid while taking the medication, and anything else he or she tells you. Make sure your doctor knows what other medications you are taking as some drugs should not be combined. If you have any questions about your medication, please talk to your doctor.

Anti-depressants work by altering the level of various chemicals in the brain that are used to transmit signals from neuron to neuron. If levels of the chemicals (called neurotransmitters) are low, the signal may arrive weakly or not arrive at all, and depression can result. A bereavement can bring on depression simply by exhausting the supply of neurotransmitters. In those cases, anti-depressants will work very well.

The medication can take a while to get

working, anything from two to eight weeks depending on the drug. After you have got past that time, you may begin to see some effects. Sometimes it is necessary to change medication to find one that works best, though you will need to be past the "not working" stage to assess this. Anti-depressants may have to be taken for months, or even years. Your doctor will advise you on how long to take them in your own case.

Side effects are likely to be foremost in people's minds when they are prescribed medication. Most drugs come with a long list of potential side effects gathered as a result of clinical trials involving perhaps thousands of people.

When faced with such a list, it can be a little daunting, not to mention scary. However, you have to remember that it is unlikely that any one person will suffer all the side effects listed. Far more common would be for a person to have a select handful of side effects which probably fade after a few weeks. Your doctor can advise you about what side effects you can expect.

All the information you could possibly want on the medication you've been prescribed is out on the Web. Somewhere...

The search engines are quite a good starting place. Bear in mind that you may have to search for the ***chemical name***, not the brand name. Brand names can differ between countries (i.e. Seroxat in the UK is known as Paxil in the US), so it is worth looking under the chemical name (paroxetine in the case of Paxil/Seroxat) as that does not change.

It is also worth knowing the class of anti-depressant you are looking for, because they can work in different ways and affect different neurotransmitters. These are some of the common classes:

- SSRI – Selective Serotonin Reuptake Inhibitors
- MAOI – Monoamine Oxidase Inhibitors
- Tricyclic or tetracyclic

So many, many times messages and scriptures were such a comfort to me. These messages and scriptures matured me and caused me to rely more on God's strength and less and less on my own. Faith was and still is the key to my slow but steady climb out of the pit of fear and depression.

"For I am convinced that nothing can separate us from his love. Death can't and Life can't. The angels won't and all the powers of hell itself cannot keep His love away. Our fears for today, our worries about tomorrow, or where we are – high above the sky or in the deepest ocean –

nothing will ever be able to separate us from the will of God, demonstrated by our Lord Jesus Christ when He died for us"[24]

Romans 8:38, 39

CHAPTER 11

GROWING PAINS

There was a time in the early 1980's I think, where whenever I started to pray, the enemy would put the most vile words and phrases into my mind, and I felt powerless to stop them. I cried many tears and suffered terribly. Eventually I realized that they were coming from the devil, and I was able to ignore it, and the thoughts went away. The enemy will try anything he can to ruin our prayer life, our communication with God. In most cases, the devil doesn't have to do much. Laziness, indifference our busy schedules are normally sufficient to accomplish this.

It really helped me when the Holy Spirit let me know that all of my afflictions, bad thoughts, anxiety, fear, doubt, depression and worry were all from the enemy. He also told me to let the past be the past. He told me that He would heal all of the memories and make them as though they never happened. He would take the memories away.

My favorite scripture was found in the early 1980's.

"Ask and it shall be given you; seek and you shall find; knock and it shall be opened unto you:

For every one that asketh, receiveth; and he that seeketh, findeth; and to him that knocketh it shall be opened.

Or what man is there of you, whom if his son ask bread, will give him a stone?

Or if he ask a fish, will he give him a serpent?

If ye then, being evil, know how to give good gifts unto your children, how much more shall your Father which is in heaven give good things to them that ask Him?"[1]

Matthew 7:7-11

I asked God for eternal life, forgiveness of sins and the Holy Spirit's Guidance. So I received them. Anyone who is sorry for their sins and accepts Jesus as their Lord and Savior and wants to be saved will be saved. My faith is so strong now that not only do I believe everything Jesus said, I know that everything Jesus said is true. I know that I know. My pastor, Dr. Kevin Baird, says that he has a 'knower", and he knows from his "knower". I understand what he's talking about.

The Holy Spirit told me that since I believe everything that Jesus said, some of which gave me a healthy fear of the Lord, that I will have everlasting life, and that I have the guidance of the Holy Spirit. He told me that this entire episode of depression in my life was a test of my faith in which I fought a mighty battle against the enemy, and that I am victorious. He told me that now it was a painful memory and that He would heal it.

I wrote in my journal December 18, 1984…"Started over with a new life. I learned about a kind, loving, merciful God who forgives if only we ask. We don't have to do anything else. Jesus paid the price. We do, however need to see a change in our lives. In this new life (new creation) we don't have to worry about the future."

I learned that Satan had been responsible for all of my misery and suffering, but God has used it for good. I know that I'm going to heaven.

I wrote in my journal December 24, 1984…"The Lord told me that I need to live one day at a time and to have a sense of humor. (something that I often forget) He has given me the means to have a good life on earth."

CHAPTER 12

MY FAMILY

"One of your greatest blessings is your family," God told me. This was so true. It is indescribable the importance of my family. In the initial stages of my depression, before I was saved, they were the main reasons I kept going on daily. Their love was an awesome anchor in my life. I remember one night as I was crying in our bedroom, I told Barbara not to let them see me in the condition I was in. I didn't want that out of shame and embarrassment, and I realized the insecurity it could cause them to feel. And even after I was saved, God let me know how important this was. Numerous occasions they were the motivating factor in my life. For example I would work in the yard, usually feeling the weight of the whole world on my shoulder. At the end of the day, I would come in take a shower and cuddle up on the sofa with Barbara, Jared and Joey, often watching Christian shows for children. That is another way that my depression was a real blessing to me. Partly because of my depression, I had very little distractions to take up my time. Most of my time was devoted, as it should be, to my family. Barbara and I really used this time to build the spiritual foundation for our kids. We'd have a devotional time where I would read a story from "Little Visits With God", and then we'd discuss it. Those were the best times in the middle of my depressed years. They would make me laugh and I'd make them laugh. And Barbara, I can't say enough about her. She stuck with me; she encouraged me, and trusted that God would bring me out of the "pit". There were bath times, play time, discipline times, and bedtimes. I would not change one thing of my life.

On weekends there were morning baseball games and soccer games and then the rest of the day at the beach, fun in the sun. It's hard not to get a lift after days like that, and getting outside in the sun and being active had its obvious physiological and psychological benefits.

Since my life was centered on Jesus and revolved around my family, my relationship with Barbara, Jared and Joey blossomed and grew stronger. They are so much a part of me, and their unconditional love and devotion factored into my recovery. Some miracles are sudden and some occur over a period of time. My miracle was of the latter variety, but I wouldn't have had it any other way.

We went to Walt Disney World two or three times during summer vacations. The kids had a blast, Barbara had a blast and I enjoyed it as much as possible. In 1988, I finally went to Disney world without being under a cloud of depression. It was great.

Your marriage is really put to the test during periods of depression. Remember your wedding vows, the part where you say, "In good times and in bad, in sickness and in health, til death do us part?" Periods of depression are the "bad and the sick". This is a tough time for your spouse, seeing you with a long face day after day, the crying, and witnessing the withdrawal from everyday life. This is when the faint of heart pack their bags. This is why Christ has to be the center of you marriage and the center of your life. If He is the anchor of your soul then you won't give up. You will seek Him with all your heart, you will stand on His promises, and you will get medical help (physical healing) if needed. Don't turn your nose up at anti-depression drugs! God put the healing in those chemicals otherwise you might as well be eating dirt. Don't limit God by your own limitations!

Try to find something each day to look forward to. It's hard, but you can do it, while you're healing. I found peace and solitude in my family, that's what I looked forward to. This is one reason to pick a soul mate whose beauty is more than skin deep. Barbara is a beautiful woman, but is beautiful on the inside as well. A shallow person is not going to be very understanding in turbulent times. You know we would all like for life to be smooth with no bumps, but the Lord told me very plainly, "Every part of your life cannot be perfect all of the time."

Today, my two boys say they don't remember me being depressed, so I am glad of that. I did a good job of insuring that they weren't affected, I guess.

The Holy Spirit told me, "When you defeat Satan, you have defeated all of his army. Just as when a general surrenders, his entire army surrenders. You have defeated the spirit of doubt, the spirit of confusion, the spirit of fear, the spirit of worry, the sprit of fear and the spirit of depression."

"God is Master of the Scriptures." This was very important to me, to know that Jesus would say whatever He wanted.

"God will not refuse any good thing that you ask of Him in Jesus' Name. Forgiveness, eternal life and the Holy Spirit's guidance are good things."

"So that anyone who believes in Me will have eternal life."[1]

John 3:15

"He that believeth on Him is not condemned."[2]

John 3:18

I am righteous not because of anything that I have done, but because of what God has done through me through Jesus His Son, and by the power of the Holy Spirit.

I wrote, “God has shown His love for me by putting together the broken pieces of my life and making me a new creation. God has also shown His love for me by letting me know that my prostate trouble is caused by my kidney stones.”

God told me, “Listen to God not man. One example is the prostate pamphlet. It is some theory by a doctor. Each time God heals your prostate, it is totally healed.” You see, I picked up this pamphlet in the doctors office, actually my doctor gave it to me, and it was supposed to give me some insight into my prostate trouble. In my state of mind at the time, I took everything in the worst possible way, and it seemed to say that I could have some deep-seated infection that would never be entirely gone. To me this meant, I could have picked up something while I was in Viet-Nam. This bothered me for years, until God delivered me, until I started listening to God rather than man. Does this mean that I quit taking advice and listening to counsel? No of course not. But it did mean that life's sticky problems and dilemmas required more than man's insight. I was listening to God as the final word. Looking back I realize how many times God delivered me from situations, problems that almost seemed impossible to overcome. But God always comes through by His Word and His Spirit. And Jesus is the Word made Flesh.

These two poems helped me tremendously and kind of summed up how I felt at the time and still feel to this day.

O REJOICE IN THE LORD

God never moves without purpose or plan
When trying his servant or molding a man
Give thanks to the Lord though His testing seems long
In darkness He giveth a song

O rejoice in the Lord, He makes no mistake
He knoweth the end of each path that I take
For when I am tried and purified
I shall come forth as gold

I could not see through the shadows ahead
So I looked at the cross of my Savior instead

I bowed to the will of the Master that day
Then peace came and tears fled away

Now I can see that testing comes from above
God strengthens His children and purges with love
My father knows best and I trust in His care
Through purging more fruit will I bear

Author unknown

IN THE CENTER OF HIS CIRCLE

In the center of the Circle
Of the will of God I stand
There come no second causes
All must come from His dear hand
All is well, Tis my Father
Who my life hath planned

Shall I pass through waves of sorrow
Then I know it will be best
Though I cannot tell the reason
I can trust so am blest

God is love and God is faithful
So in perfect peace I rest
With the shade and with the sunshine
With the joy and with the pain
Lord I trust the both are needed
Each thy wayward children to train
Earthly loss did we but know it
Often means our heavenly gain

Author unknown

Worrying about material things is the biggest waste of time. Don't let it take you twenty or thirty years to figure that out. People worry about the silliest things. I've stressed out over a beautiful lawn. I've worked at it for over thirty years and it still doesn't look much better than it did when I started. There are weeds, bugs, fungus and moles. I've been a perfectionist most of my life, stressing out over anything I did when it didn't turn out perfect. This is why I never expect perfection out of anyone else; in fact I've told them so. But I'm not going to let perfectionism plague me the rest of my days. I've come to see how blest I really am. I see the big picture.

Miracles don't always happen suddenly, as I've said before. My pastor, Dr. Kevin Baird, said that the word "suddenly" is said only fourty-one times in the Bible. "And it came to pass" is said over four hundred times. Miracles happen over a period of time almost ten times more than those suddenly. The miracle in my life has been ongoing for thirty years. I prayed to have my life back, I prayed to be a good husband and father and I prayed to have the peace that passeth all understanding. These miracles happened because I had instructions from the Bible, I believed those instructions, I launched my boat and let down my nets and came up with a net full of miracles. But my miracles took time, they came to pass. Yours will too if you believe what Jesus said.

God wants us to expect good things in life, not bad things, but He doesn't want us to fall apart when bad things happen. He doesn't want us to worry. He wants us to expect Him to take care of our every need.

"What a wonderful God we have. He is the Father of our Lord Jesus Christ, the source of every mercy and the One who so wonderfully comforts and strengthens us in our hardships and our trials. And why does He do this? So that when others are troubled, needing our sympathy and encouragement, we can pass on the same help and comfort God has given us. You can be sure that the more we undergo sufferings for Christ, the more He will shower us

with His comfort and encouragement."[3]

The reason that I have written this book is not merely to sympathize, but to give comfort to those suffering from depression fear and worry; hopefully to shorten the "learning curve" for others from my experiences. I believe that God wanted me to write these things and I believe that that is one of the reasons that I went through them. You need to know that you are more than overcomers through Christ.

I wrote in my journal, "I am winning victory after victory, because I have the Holy Spirit. I give all the credit to God." That being said, when you need a miracle in your life, it usually takes an action on your part, a lot of hard work and follow through.

One thing that meant so much to me and continues to be, and even more so is the fact that when your sins are forgiven, it's as though they never happened. This was a burst of light into the darkness for me. I am a new creation and can be finally rid of the past.

God is all kind and all understanding. He does not want you to worry all day about whether or not you committed sins. But rather, at the end of each day, talk to Him and tell Him that you are sorry for your sins and for offending Him in any way. I'm not saying be cavalier about sinning, I'm saying if you are sorry God will forgive you.

CHAPTER 13

DON'T LOSE HOPE, FIND THE WILL TO LIVE AND SEE YOUR DOCTOR

Please don't give up hope in life. I know from my own experiences that life can be absolutely horrific. However, at other times it can be gloriously wonderful. It can sometimes take a while to get from the bad place to the good, but I have never regretted sticking this journey out to get there. Please hear me out and give yourself a chance. Please do not end it all.

Though you may feel desperately alone and isolated, I understand your situation. Even though I do not know you personally, I care. Also, I know that God cares. Because I know God exists, and cares for everyone, I know that whoever you are and whatever your circumstance, there is always hope if you reach out to God and recognize his reality. However you feel about yourself, he knows you, and your situation, and he wants to help. He forgives whatever we have done wrong, and is present everywhere. He never turns down someone who calls on him.

As I have already said, if you feel suicidal, then you must be in a very difficult personal circumstance or state. It is not really possible to list all of the problems or situations which may have contributed to how you feel, and why your situation is as serious as it seems. What I do want to do is to provide as much help and encouragement to you as possible. I hope that this book will continue to be a source of hope and strength for you in the future, as you persevere and move forward in hope.

If you are a Christian, you already believe in God, and I trust have known him as a friend and a source of meaning and strength to you in your life. Most sensible people know that knowing God does not disclude them from trouble and strife. The strife may or may not be in part of your own making. Perhaps you are a victim of wrong doing (for example, rape or bullying), which has had a profound negative affect on you. Because of your deep personal misery, and/or to get out of a difficult situation you have found yourself in, you may feel that you would be happier dead than living. Life is so terrible, that you want an end to the suffering.

These feelings happen to a significant number of people. Anyone can be affected; rich or poor, young or old, Christian or non-Christian. Don't feel guilty if you a Christian and you feel suicidal. I know that there will be reasons. Whatever the reasons, the devil is likely to be exaggerating your problems (and any areas of spiritual weakness), making things even harder. I deal with this spiritual dynamic a little more below. However, whatever the circumstance, and recognizing that there will be valid reasons for why you feel the way that you do, this does not mean that you have a right to take your own life.

God gave you life, so let him take it at the right time. Whether you die from age or from an illness, or whatever, allow him to be in control of your destiny. Trust him. Meanwhile, take pressure off of yourself. Live for God, and try to find Him. When you get through this time, show kindness to others in need, and know the fact that God can use you. Also, realize how special you are to him.

I want to acknowledge the deep feelings of pain and desperation that people can be subject to when they suffer. Perhaps you have always been unhappy, as long as you can remember. As well as neglectful or abusive parents, perhaps you were bullied at school. All that you have experienced is rejection, and even if you are a Christian and have regularly gone to Church, perhaps you found different types of abuse and rejection there.

Only God knows the fullness of your situation and how you feel about it. I want to offer two things; first of all some information about places that you can go to for help. Secondly, I want to encourage you to turn to God, and to Christians and others (for example, a local doctor), whom you feel you can trust, for help.

Hopefully, some of what I have already shared with you sounds a little familiar to you; and you may be considering reading the rest of my story. As well as this, consider talking to a doctor about the basic things that are troubling you. It could be that there is a medical reason for your depression or suicidal thoughts. Professional counseling may be very beneficial in getting to the root cause of your problem, and you can carefully access with your counselor the reasons for your negative feelings. If you have helpful friends, use them to support you, and if you go to church, ask for help there.

Even if your church cannot provide proper counseling, it should be able to provide some form of support. Consider changing churches if it cannot, and ask your new church how strong their pastoral ministry is, and if they will provide some form of support. Sharing your problems with others may really help you. Their listening and perhaps their advice, may somehow "meet you where you need to be met."

"Suicide is usually a shocking surprise to family and friends who then only realize how serious things were. Over and over the stunned survivors ask, "What went wrong?" --- not understanding that the person was sick. It wasn't just stress, or a wrong choice. It was an illness called depression, outside one's self-control, capable of overwhelming any of us. People in great despair sometimes try to free themselves from depression through intense and sincere spiritual effort. Well-meaning friends may compound their friend's agony by telling them that some discipline or experience they have not yet had will lift them from the pit. Such methods are wrong-headed because they fail to treat the cause of the illness. They are also dangerous because, in failing, they prolong the sickness and risk a fatal termination.

Do real Christians get depressed? You bet they do. My own perspective is that my patients, including my Christian patients, do best when they adopt exactly the same attitude toward the chemical solutions that modern medicine has adopted for their depression as they have for the medicines they take for hypertension, diabetes, or pneumonia. Seeing people rediscover purpose, meaning and joy through this means makes it clear to me that these medical interventions should be viewed as God's allies, for if I understand His Word correctly, He desires the very same things, (as sense of purpose, meaning and joy) to all who trust in Him."[1]

Chapter 14

Turn to God for help, Standing Firm Against the enemy, bitterness and Unforgiveness.

As well as these practical measures, turn to God for help. Pray and fast, asking for the Lord to answer your prayers and lift off the heaviness that you feel. Also, believe in Scripture, that God is able to help you and heal you. Isaiah 53:1-12, is very useful. Verse 5 says..."He was pierced for our transgressions, he was crushed for our iniquities; the punishment that bought us peace was upon him, and by his wounds we are healed."[1] Jesus died to heal us of the hurt that is caused by our own sin (wrong or immoral thoughts or actions), the sin done to us, and the effect of sin in the world. You should examine yourself before God, and truly repent of any sin if you have not already done so.

I would also like to add that as well as turning to God, and drawing our strength from him, we very much have to hold on to hope ourselves. God can and will help us, but survival will often require courage and an ability to valiantly stand. This is despite fear, suffering and perhaps confusion, which all act to try to undermine.

"Lord, these are days when the craftiest hunter and trapper around doesn't display his license or sport a glowing orange cap and vest. Sharp and skilled at every sneaking device, he stalks and snares the souls of men. I'd not venture out without a prayer to keep me from the evil one. And I would ask for the safe return to rest within my Father's sanctuary."

Author Unknown

In my experience, the devil can make matters much worse – when you are already suffering in some way. I feel that often he can have a direct contribution to the burdens of some people, troubling their minds and emotions with all sorts of negative and evil thoughts and feelings. There are several good books available about this area.

Mental disorders can be a significant contributory factor to cause suicidal feelings. I would also like to make clear that there are many other, more natural, reasons why people can feel suicidal. Perhaps they have experienced intense loneliness and a lack of friends for some time. When a practical solution has been found to a problem like this, for example, a better social environment is discovered, then if the enemy has been exploiting the problem, his influence will be reduced as normality is restored. There is less for the enemy to latch on to.

I would like to warn people that there are some Christian teachers and Christian ministries which over-emphasize, in my opinion, the part that the demonic can play in causing Christians problems. This can be very dangerous and negative to people's well-being. The attitude of some is that demons can be caught almost as easily as catching a cold. It is unhealthy to focus on demons. When they are causing us problems, we should recognize this and not deny it. I feel that we should not assume that people are demonized. We should probe, and challenge any darkness, but it is wrong to place demons on people. Perhaps the enemy could even use this sort of negatively-focused environment as an opportunity to multiply any influence he does have on the ministered-to individual.

If you feel that you are in a serious spiritual battle against the enemy, use both fellowship support and also your own authority in Christ to stand against demonic oppression. You have the Word of God at your disposal, so use its truth to combat lies and other attacks. For example, you know from reading the Bible that nothing can separate (you) from the love of God that is in Christ

Jesus. (Romans 8:38, 39).[2] Neither angels nor demons nor anything in creation. However, it should be added at this point that this is true as long as we do not persist in any particular sin, and leave it unrepented. This puts us on shaky ground, and leaves us exposed to enemy influence.

The enemy really messed with my prayer life for a time. He exploited a new area in my life that was unavailable for so long because I hardly ever prayed except at bedtime sometimes. It was almost as if the enemy figured that if I'd found him out finally, that he was the culprit in so many things; he was going to make me even more miserable. He began to put vulgar thoughts and foul language in my mind while I prayed, and you can't just force thoughts out of your mind, so I had to ignore it. I wasn't going to stop praying just because of this little maneuver. But oh, it hurt so bad for a time. You're trying to communicate with God and these thoughts are trying to flood your mind. But after a time, they went away and how I praised God. It felt good to stand firm and hold my ground and not give up something precious to me and my God.

There are some that would argue this is why it's not good for people to be aware of the devil because it opens them up to fears and manipulations by him, but that's just not correct. You must be aware of him. You can't just stick your head in the sand and hope he'll go away. For me, sure I struggled, but it's just like handling a bully. You have to stand up to him; except that in the case of the devil you must stand up to him with God at your side. You don't want to try doing it alone. Actually, it was a relief to me when I realized that I wasn't an evil person, dreaming up all of these disgusting thoughts and words while I was trying to pray. Life began to make more sense as I realized the spiritual battle that we're all in.

"The enemy plans the dark valley that will take away everything we have; God allows us to pass through it so that He can give us more eternal gifts and promises than we can carry."[3]

The Holy Spirit told me one day, "All of the misery you have experienced has come from the enemy. I will heal all of your memories of this misery and make it as though it never happened. I will take all of the memories away."

God's Word gave me many comforting scriptures.

Looking back to my footprints, I see where I staggered through a minefield, but You guided my stumbling feet.

I teetered on the edge of a precipice; but You kept Your promise to keep me from falling.

I skirted a pond of quicksand and was stopped

on the edge of a swamp. Goodness and mercy were following me.

And from a song…Through many dangers toils and snares, I have already come…And now I walk the King's Highway that leads me home.

I want to say a word about bitterness. The hurtful actions and words of others may be at the root of some of your problems. Perhaps part of your suffering has been caused by the sin that others have done against you. A good example of this is when someone has sexually abused you as a child. It is so important to forgive people like this who have wronged us.

Even when this is incredibly hard, we must commit ourselves to forgive. This is often a process that takes time. You may begin by reaching a point where you are prepared to forgive someone in principal – out of obedience and fear of God (Matthew 5:21-25).[4] Real forgiveness does need to come, however, even if it is released gradually.

If the person who has wronged us is still known to us, and perhaps seen by us regularly, this can make things all the harder. However, we must forgive to be reconciled with God, and to enable him to heal us fully. As bitterness leaves us, hurt can be dealt with. Mary Pytches, a well-known Christian author, describes forgiveness as a key principal towards inner healing and wholeness.

Whatever the reason for your suffering, you are not alone. So many people, including many Christians, suffer in different ways around the world. Feeling anger towards those who wrong us is normal, but do turn to God for help to forgive people. He also offers us the hope that we can again – or for the first time, know real happiness and peace in our lives. I hope and pray that you know that peace, and the true comfort of Christ.

Chapter 15

Getting over it, Getting it and Getting better

As I mentioned earlier, many things happened to me while I was in Viet-Nam, but nothing over there caused my depression. My construction platoon was shot at and pinned down by Viet Cong preparing for an assault, but two Cobras bailed us out. Another time I had an entire squad wounded from minor scratches to major wounds requiring hospitalization (but no fatalities). And I knew of heart-wrenching problems in my men from drug addictions to dear-John letters from home. None of which I could do a thing about. I didn't know Jesus then, not really, as I wasn't saved.

But something I did hurt me later far worse than any bullet wound or other physical hurt. I had wanted for Barbara and I to be virgins when we got married, not that I was worried about her. While I was in Bangkok, Thailand on R&R, (Rest and Relaxation), a prostitute was brought to my hotel room by a cab driver. He was trying to sell me a massage. I was minding my own business reading a book, but I let her in. It took me a long time to get over the disappointment. The enemy used it against me many times, but God's Word says all manner of sin shall be forgiven unto man. Barbara forgave me, but I was such a perfectionist and so chemically disposed to get depressed that it was hard to get over. I know this will sound silly to a lot of people, knowing that many men went through such awful experiences in battle and came home maimed physically and mentally and emotionally.

Worrying became a way of life for me for a long time.

I worried about whether I was getting the right amount of anti-depressant medication.

I worried about whether I installed a dimmer switch properly. It was more than worrying, it was obsessing.

I worried that I caused a chip on an antique bottle.

I worried about my structural designs. (They're all still standing).

God brought me through all of these obsessive thoughts. The Holy Spirit spoke to me in 1986, "You must trust God completely and turn things over to Him. Someday, if something happens to you that you can't handle, where will you be if you don't know how to turn things over to God? This will help you to remain joyful through all things." So I surrendered finally. There will always be struggles, but the Holy Spirit told me that I was no longer under bondage. Be inspired by history, don't be trapped by it. True wisdom comes from the Holy Spirit. So I surrendered my life to God and quit trying to do everything on my own, and the peace that I felt passed all understanding. I knew by the Holy Spirit that I was no longer under bondage and that God wanted me to be happy. He said when I pray it's my decision; He's not interested in a certain quantity of prayer like trying to fill a quota.

I can't overemphasize the importance of keeping a journal. My recommendation is a spiral bound, and I would write in pencil so that you can erase instead of crossing out. Keep a pencil and paper in the car. Sometimes you may get a word from the Lord while you're in the car. Just remember what it is and the next time that you stop you can safely write it down. If you forget it or do not have paper and pencil, do not fret. He will bring it back to you memory, if you really need it. The reason a journal is important, well there are many reasons that a journal is important, but one of them is so that you can look back and see the progress you've made. Another reason that a journal is important is that you have captured that thought from the Holy Spirit, or that special scripture that opened your eyes to the Truth. Invariably you will have the same battle facing you somewhere down the line and you will be able to look back and see how the Holy Spirit helped you to be victorious the last time. You will almost imperceptibly become an overcomer. For myself, I have overcome much, especially fears of all sorts. There are times, however when the enemy rears his ugly head and brings up the old torments and I struggle chemically. I guess it's the human condition, well not for everyone, but for many. Christian or non-Christian, the enemy will attack us in our mind and we need to realize that sickness of the body came to us because of sin. Depression came into this world because of sin.

The Bible tells us that there is no struggle that others have not already gone through and that's important for us to know. We often think that the struggle that we're going through is unique. We feel that we're all alone in it and that the situation is hopeless. The fact is there is no situation that we go through that is outside the power of God to solve. God's Word is miraculous. I have never been in a struggle that God has not brought me out of by His Word and His Spirit. No circumstance do I fear because I know that God will get me through it. He's done it by other ways as well. I've turned on the car radio and a Christian speaker will say something that I needed to hear; or a song will come on and the lyrics are just what I needed to hear.

One pitfall that I'd rather not see you fall into is the habit of over-reasoning, (because you'll have to climb out). There are times when you must accept God's Word as it is written and don't continue to look at the circumstances trying to reason it out. (Talk about chasing your tail.) Jesus said, "Man does not live by bread alone but by every word that comes from the mouth of God."[1]

Matthew 4:4

God's wonderful healing powers are available to us through doctor's and prescription drugs. This bothers some people who feel guilty that they are not relying fully on God. Some of these same people though will take medication for their heart, cholesterol, acne, headaches, cancer, kidney stones and list goes on. It's alright to take prescription medication for depression. Don't limit God and refuse his help. Jesus had compassion on hurting people and healed <u>*all*</u> of their afflictions. That bothered people back then who didn't think it was right for one reason or another. It didn't say that it bothered anyone that was healed though. If God's healing power were not in those chemicals, you may as well be eating dirt. If you break a leg, don't you put a cast on it? If you have a tumor in your body, don't you let a doctor remove it? God has given man the ability to do these things, so certainly you may go to a doctor for anti-depressant drugs.

"We realize that some Christian counselors and pastors teach that using anything other than the Bible, faith and the Holy Spirit's power to overcome life's difficulties, including depression is wrong. If depression were purely an issue of the spirit we would have no problem with this assertion. However since depression is a whole person issue, it is rarely a purely spiritual matter. What affects us spiritually affects us psychologically, sociologically and physically and vice versa.

We expect that those who promote the idea that depression should only be treated by the Bible and faith have never spent time with Christians struggling with serious psychological disorders whether in a psychiatric ward or outside. Had they done so they might not be so quick to deny the value of pharmacological intervention in some cases."[2]

"While I'm on the subject of anti-depressant drugs, I'm going to tell you about my experience with them. I am not a doctor so what I'm telling you is general information based on my experience with them. There are many available that were not on the market when I started taking them. The more popular are Zoloft, Welbutrin and Prozac. My doctor prescribed Amitriptyline (Elavil). He told me that he would start with that because it helped the most people. If he found that it didn't help, he would try another until he hit the right one. You have to be patient. My doctor was a psychiatrist that my family doctor recommended. You have to give the medication a chance to work; it's not a "happy pill". It's a medication that gives you the will to work through your depression and whatever triggered it. It does this by balancing chemicals in your brain, which through no fault of your own have gotten out of balance. I really didn't have to see a psychiatrist for therapy, I just had to go to him to write a prescription and that's who my family doctor recommended. Today my new family doctor writes the refills. Family physicians have much more knowledge and options than they did thirty years ago.

In about a month I started to feel some relief, and in six months I felt better than what had been normal for me. However I had not progressed one inch spiritually. That was a whole new battle to fight. In a about a month after getting off of the anti depressants tiny things started to bother me and eventually the perfectionism returned and the ridiculous and obsessive things. Looming fears and a lack of happiness, for no apparent reason let me know that I needed help again. My old family doctor retired and I started going to a younger guy about my age and he really helped me. He told me how common depression was and how many people he saw for treatment. It's hard for me to imagine suffering from depression and not seeking help. Many people that don't get help turn to alcohol, drugs or worse.

"If you believe the use of anti-depressant medications will enable you to function more normally and may increase your ability to ponder the deeper issues of the heart that may be related to your depression, then you should seek the help of both a Christian physician and a Christian counselor (or counselors) who are willing and able to help you to press on toward the mark of the higher calling of God in Christ Jesus (see Phil. 3:12-14). In the end, whatever you decide, the main thing worth taking from your experience with depression is the deeper knowledge that real hope is only found in one place – an ever-deepening relationship with Christ, who understands the depths of our pain and died to heal it all."[3]

The Holy Spirit told me, "Every time Satan tries to tell you one of his lies, you know that God has already told you the truth about these situations. He has told you that Satan is lying. So there is no reason to think about these lies anymore."

These are some messages from the Holy Spirit that I received in 1986 that really helped to jump start me spiritually.

"Don't try to figure out what God reveals to you; accept it."

"God wants you to know that He loves you and that I will reveal the meaning of scriptures as you need it."

When you believe God's Word it changes your life, I am living proof of that. I was the weakest of the weak, but God's strength shows up best in weak people. So the weaker I was the stronger I became and it is all God's strength. Colossians 2:12 says that we have new lives because we trusted the Word of God who raised Christ from the dead.[4]

CHAPTER 16

NEVER GIVE UP

Please, when battling depression, never give up. It is a physical condition no different than any other illness of the body, except that it is more confounding because it affects the mind and the emotions. It has to be understood that depression is caused by an imbalance of chemicals in the brain. It's probably been the cause of many diagnoses of alcoholism. Alcohol and illegal drugs mask the symptoms of depression, but anti-depressants rebalance the chemicals and help us fight our way out of depression and its debilitating effects. Depression is treatable and the drugs nowadays are truly miracles from God. Just ask anyone who has escaped that downward spiral and returned to live a normal life. The longer you have suffered from depression, the longer it takes to get back to normal, but stay steadfast in your resolve and never give up. You can and you will make it. It may take six weeks or it may take six months, but you will prevail. When the psychiatrist told me that it would take me six months to feel normal again, I was aghast. I thought there was no way I could stand it. But when he told me that I would feel a little better in three or four weeks, that was a little more encouraging. Some days you may not feel like you made much progress. Some days you may feel like you regressed, but some days you'll feel like you're almost there. Realize that there are millions of people like yourself that have struggled like you, you're not alone. You're not alone in this battle and you're not the only person that's ever been this messed up. Remember that the Bible says that no one goes through anything that hasn't been a trial for someone already.

CHAPTER 17

GOD'S HEALING DIRT

Here I have listed some information on Antidepressant Medications Anti-depressant Drugs, side effects, depression, MAO, SSRI, Tricyclics, symptoms of Depression, treatment. The kind of depression that will most likely benefit from treatment with medications is more than just "the blues." It's a condition that's prolonged, lasting 2 weeks or more, and interferes with a person's ability to carry on daily tasks and to enjoy activities that previously brought pleasure. The depressed person will seem sad, or "down," or may show a lack of interest in his surroundings. They may have trouble eating and lose weight (although some people eat more and gain weight when depressed). They may sleep too much or too little, have difficulty going to sleep, sleep restlessly, or awaken very early in the morning. They may speak of feeling guilty, worthless, or hopeless. They may complain that their thinking is slowed down. They may lack energy, feeling "everything's too much," or they might be agitated and jumpy. A person who is depressed may cry. They may think and talk about ending it all and may even make a suicide attempt. Some people who are depressed have psychotic symptoms, such as delusions (false ideas) that are related to their depression. For instance, a psychotically depressed person might imagine that he is already dead, or "in hell," being punished. Not everyone who is depressed has all these symptoms, but everyone who is depressed has at least some of them. A depression can range in intensity from mild to severe. Antidepressants are used most widely for serious depressions, but they can also be helpful for some milder depressions. Antidepressants, although they are not "uppers" or stimulants, take away or reduce the symptoms of depression and help the depressed person feel the way he did before he became depressed. Anti-depressants are largely misunderstood by many. They err in thinking that anti-depressants are similar to recreational drugs like cocaine; or that they're tranquilizers of some sort that just keep you subdued. No this is far from the truth. While they do help in this way, it's just enough to help you want to battle the depression and come out of it. It's a fight that takes a lot of courage and character, and a fight that's worth it by the way.

Antidepressants are also used for disorders characterized principally by anxiety. They can block the symptoms of panic, including rapid heartbeat, terror, dizziness, chest pains, nausea, and breathing problems. They can also be used to treat some phobias. The physician chooses the particular antidepressant to prescribe based on the individual patient's symptoms. When someone begins taking an antidepressant, improvement generally will not begin to show immediately. With most of these medications, it will take from 1 to 3 weeks before changes begin to occur. Some symptoms diminish early in treatment; others, later. For instance, a person's energy level or sleeping or eating patterns may improve before his depressed mood lifts. If there is little or no change in symptoms after 5 to 6 weeks, a different medication may be tried. Some people will respond better to one than another. Since there is no certain way of determining beforehand which medication will be effective, the doctor may have to prescribe first one, then another, until an effective one is found. Treatment is continued for a minimum of several months and may last up to a year or more. While some people have one episode of depression and then never have another, or remain symptom-free for years, others have more frequent episodes or very long-lasting depressions that may go on for years. Some people find that their depressions become more frequent and severe as they get older. For these people, continuing (maintenance) treatment with antidepressants can be an effective way of reducing the frequency and severity of depressions. Those that are commonly used have no known long-term side effects and may be continued indefinitely. The prescribed dosage of the medication may be lowered if side effects become troublesome. Lithium can also be used for maintenance treatment of repeated depressions whether or not there is evidence of a manic or manic-like episode in the past. Dosage of antidepressants varies, depending on the type of drug, the person's body chemistry, age, and, sometimes, body weight. Dosages are generally started low and raised gradually over time until the desired effect is reached without the appearance of troublesome side effects. There are a number of antidepressant medications available. They differ in their side effects and, to some extent, in their level of effectiveness. Tricyclic antidepressants (named for their chemical structure) are more commonly used for treatment of major depressions than are monoamine oxidase inhibitors (MAOIs); but MAOIs are often helpful in so-called "atypical" depressions in which there are symptoms like oversleeping, anxiety, panic attacks, and phobias. The last few years have seen the introduction of a number of new antidepressants. Several of them are called "selective serotonin reuptake inhibitors" (SSRIs). Those available at the present time in the United States are fluoxetine (Prozac), fluvoxamine (Luvox), paroxetine (Paxil) (my anti-depressant for the last couple of years), and sertraline (Zoloft). (Luvox has been approved for obsessive-compulsive disorder, and Paxil has been approved for panic disorder.) Though structurally different from each other, all the SSRIs' antidepressant effects are due to their action on one specific neurotransmitter, serotonin. Two other antidepressants that affect two neurotransmitters, serotonin and norepinephrine, have also been approved by the FDA. They are venlafaxine (Effexor) and nefazodone (Serzone). All of these newer antidepressants seem to have less bothersome side effects than the older tricyclic antidepressants. The tricyclic antidepressant clomipramine (Anafranil) affects serotonin but is not as selective as the SSRIs. It was the first medication specifically approved for use in the treatment of obsessive compulsive disorder (OCD). Prozac and Luvox have now been approved for use with OCD. Another of the newer antidepressants, bupropion (Wellbutrin), is chemically unrelated to the other antidepressants. It has more effect on norepinephrine and dopamine than on serotonin. Wellbutrin has not been associated with weight gain or sexual dysfunction. It is contraindicated for individuals with, or at risk for, a seizure disorder or who have been diagnosed with bulimia or anorexia nervosa.

Side Effects of Antidepressant Medications

1. Tricyclic Antidepressants There are a

number of possible side effects with tricyclic antidepressants that vary, depending on the medication. For example, amitriptyline (Elavil, my anti depressant for thirty years) may make people feel drowsy, while protriptyline (Vivactil) hardly does this at all, and in some people, may have an opposite effect, producing feelings of anxiety and restlessness. Because of this kind of variation in side effects, one antidepressant might be highly desirable for one person and not recommended for another. Tricyclics on occasion may complicate specific heart problems, and for this reason the physician should be aware of all such difficulties. Other side effects with tricyclics may include blurred vision, dry mouth, constipation, weight gain, dizziness when changing position, increased sweating, difficulty urinating, changes in sexual desire, decrease in sexual ability, muscle twitches, fatigue, and weakness. Not all these medications produce all side effects, and not everybody gets them. Some will disappear quickly, while others may remain for the length of treatment. Some side effects are similar to symptoms of depression (for instance, fatigue and constipation). For this reason, the patient or family should discuss all symptoms with the doctor, who may change the medication or dosage. Tricyclics also may interact with thyroid hormone, antihypertensive medications, oral contraceptives, some blood coagulants, some sleeping medications, antipsychotic medications, diuretics, antihistamines, aspirin, bicarbonate of soda, vitamin C, alcohol, and tobacco. An overdose of antidepressants is serious and potentially lethal. It requires immediate medical attention. Symptoms of an overdose of tricyclic antidepressant medication develop within an hour and may start with rapid heartbeat, dilated pupils, flushed face, and agitation, and progress to confusion, loss of consciousness, seizures, irregular heart beats, cardiorespiratory collapse, and death.

2. The Newer Antidepressants

The most common side effects of these antidepressants are gastrointestinal problems and headache. Others are insomnia, anxiety, and agitation. Because of potentially serious interaction between these medications and monoamine oxidase inhibitors, it is advisable to stop taking one medication from 2 to 4 or 5 weeks before starting the other, depending on the specific medications involved. In addition, some SSRIs have been found to affect metabolism of certain other medications in the liver, creating possible drug interactions.

3. Monoamine Oxidase Inhibitors (MAOIs)

MAOIs may cause some side effects similar to those of the other antidepressants. Dizziness when changing position and rapid heartbeat are common. MAOIs also react with certain foods and alcoholic beverages (such as aged cheeses, foods containing monosodium glutamate (MSG), Chianti and other red wines), and other medications (such as over-the-counter cold and allergy preparations, local anesthetics, amphetamines, insulin, some narcotics, and antiparkinsonian medications). These reactions often do not appear for several hours. Signs may include severe high blood pressure, headache, nausea, vomiting, rapid heartbeat, possible confusion, psychotic symptoms, seizures, stroke, and coma. For this reason, people taking MAOIs must stay away from restricted foods, drinks, and medications. They should be sure that they are furnished, by their doctor or pharmacist, a list of all foods, beverages, and other medications that should be avoided.[1]

Sometimes the doctor will try a variety of antidepressants before finding the most effective medication or combination of medications. Sometimes the dosage must be increased to be effective. As in my case, my family doctor prescribed 50 mg of Elavil, an old but highly effective trycyclic. For months it didn't help, but when I finally saw a psychiatrist, he had me gradually increase to 250 mg and I started feeling better somewhere between 50 mg and 250 mg Although some improvements can be seen in the first few weeks, antidepressant medications must be taken regularly for 3 to 4 weeks (in some cases, as many as 8 weeks) before the full therapeutic effect occurs.

It's tempting to stop taking your medication when you start to feel better. There were a couple of times when I felt like maybe I didn't need the medication anymore. There were a lot more times that I felt like the medication wasn't working, but I can tell you that it's very important to keep taking it. And another thing, the side affects may begin before you feel better. It did in my case, although they were mild, some dry mouth and drowsiness was about it. The doctor will probably want you to stay on the medication for at least 4 to 9 months to prevent a recurrence of the depression. For me, it was 6 months, but I found out later that I would need to remain on medication for the rest of my life. I certainly wasn't crazy about that, but the alternative was unthinkable, and I became so thankful to God that there was something that could prevent a major depression. Some medications must be stopped gradually to give the body time to adjust; don't ever stop taking anti-depressant drugs without consulting the doctor for instructions on how to safely do it. For many people with bi-polar disorder or chronic major depression (that's me), medication may have to be maintained indefinitely.

Anti-depressants may cause mild and usually,

temporary side effects (sometimes referred to as adverse side effects) in some people. Typically these are annoying but not serious. However, any unusual side affects or reactions or those that interfere with functioning should be reported to the doctor immediately. The most common side effects and the way to deal with them are:

> ***Dry mouth** – it's helpful to drink sips of water; chew sugarless gum; clean teeth daily.*
>
> ***Constipation** – bran cereals, prunes, fruit, and vegetables should be in the diet.*
>
> ***Bladder problems** – emptying the bladder may be troublesome, and the urine stream may not be as strong as usual; the doctor should be notified if there is marked difficulty or pain.*
>
> ***Sexual problems** – sexual functioning may change; if worrisome it should be discussed with doctor.*
>
> ***Blurred vision** – this will pass soon and will not usually necessitate new glasses.*
>
> ***Dizziness** – rising from the bed or chair slowly is helpful.*
>
> ***Drowsiness** as a daytime problem – this usually passes soon. A person feeling drowsy or sedated should not drive or operate heavy*

equipment. The more sedating antidepressants are generally taken at bedtime to help sleep and minimize daytime drowsiness.

The newer antidepressants have different types of side effects:

***Headache** – this will usually go away.*

***Nausea** – This is also temporary, but even when it occurs it is transient after each dose.*

***Nervousness and insomnia** (trouble falling asleep or waking often during the night) – these may occur during the first few weeks; dosage reductions or time will usually resolve them.*

***Agitation** (feeling jittery) – if this happens for the first time after the drug is taken and is more transient, the doctor should be notified.*

***Sexual problems** – the doctor should be consulted if the problem is severe or worrisome.*

Precautions to be observed when taking Antidepressants

When taking antidepressants, it is important to tell all doctors (and dentists) being seen not just the one who is treating the depression about all medications being used, including over-the-counter preparations and alcohol. Antidepressants should be taken only in the amount prescribed and should be kept in a secure place away from children. When used with proper care, following doctors' instructions, antidepressants are extremely useful medications that can reverse the misery of a depression and help a person feel like himself again.[2]

"Anti-depressants do not excuse a person from changing when change is necessary. They only give people a reprieve for a little while in order to get their lives back together. If that time is wasted the depression will likely return sooner or later, perhaps more brutal than before."[3]

In their book, *New Light on Depression*, David Biebel and Harold Koenig had this to say about anti-depressant medication:

"Modern medicine and Christian counseling are also of grace. In other words, in his grace God has granted both knowledge and insight that can restore our bodies and minds of those who suffer from depression to the point where they are able to comprehend and embrace His way, unhindered by debilitating psychic and spiritual pain, which Satan can use as blinders. Thus medicine and psychotherapy can be tools in the Master's hands, not hindrances to His purposes, as long as it is acknowledged that regaining one's physical and spiritual equilibrium is the first step, not the last, in the journey toward wholeness, peace and joy that are the longing of every depressed believer."[4]

CHAPTER 18

THE EMOTIONAL WAR

Don't think that I don't know how you feel. You feel like it's hopeless, you don't enjoy the things that you used to enjoy; you no longer make plans for the future. You hate the thought of getting out of bed and having to face another day. Depression is an emotional battle. The feeling is kind of like your emotional transmission is stuck on melancholy and panic sets in because you can't get out of that gear. You see others around you enjoying life and all of life's activities. You feel really guilty because you're dragging your family down. But God is our anchor. You must trust that God is aware of your depression, but it's a part of His plan to allow you to go through this for your sake. (We'll talk more about this later.) God's Word hasn't changed. All the promises are still there. They're still for you. I think it's a good time to state again that there are at least two kinds of depression, short term and long term. Short term depression can be caused by the loss of a loved one, a failed marriage, bad news etc. These are of limited duration, and your emotions will return to normal without any assistance. Now I am not a doctor, I am writing based on what I have learned.

Don't trust your emotions. Don't trust your feelings when you are in a state of depression. Realize that it is a temporary situation and help is available. Our God is an awesome God and you will discover that physical healing is available, and you will find that there are scriptures just waiting for you to discover that are miracle-producing for your life. That's part of God's plan to seek Him through His Word. Why do you think there is a Bible? Do you think it was just some kind of exercise He was going through? No He doesn't work that way, it was for our use, our deliverance, our salvation. It is a light shining in the darkness if you will let it. You'll discover Jesus Christ and everything He said. It must have been important in order for Him to come and tell us personally. God told Him everything to say. Trust what He says not what you feel.

When you think of depression, there are multiple facets of it. We just touched on the emotional, but there are also the mental, spiritual and as we now know, the physical. I'm purposely saving the spiritual for last. The mind is an every day battlefield. Who is the attacker? Satan is correct. He is always seeking to kill and destroy us. His primary aim is to tempt us to sin, but more than that, he is trying to get us to lead and continue a life of sin. Yes we're all sinners, but we do not all make it a practice of sinning. However when we're stricken with depression, our minds are much more susceptible to Satan's deceptions. For Christians, Satan will often twist or distort scriptures into his lie. He will try to plague us with confusion, doubt and fears which all compound themselves and our imaginations can be runaway freight trains gaining momentum every day. "Emotional pain and depression have been defined by one scholar as a highly concentrated thought."[1] From my own personal experience; I think this is very astute. Often, I have dwelled on a thought for a long time, and it put me in a state of emotional turmoil that I could not escape entirely unless I faced that thought head on. Now here is an important personal observation. I have gotten out of a state of depression with God's physical healing, but until I faced that particular thought spiritually with scripture, the problem was not truly reconciled.

CHAPTER 19

THE SPIRITUAL WAR – YOU CAN'T LOSE

The mind is where Satan normally attacks Christians. For the non-believer Satan doesn't have to work very hard to get them to sin, but his assaults on their mind pales in comparison to what he will try with the believer. A true believer will not make a practice of sinning so Satan can find no inroads there. But what he can do is bring up past sins to try to accuse you with, or cause you to worry or be anxious about something that is very important to you. For a Christian, eternal salvation is very important and what better gift from our Heavenly Father could he use to cause us pain. Satan will twist scripture, he will use imaginations, irrational fears and worries to trap you into the gloomy pit of depression. For an individual with a chemical imbalance, like myself, without God's physical, emotional, mental and spiritual healing, a life of misery and pain would be all but certain. Christians are subject to mental battles just as much as much as the rest of the population, but most of them feel like something must be the matter with them. They feel that if they were where they should be spiritually, they could not be wounded so terribly in their mind. Now I am not saying that a spiritually handicapped person can not be attacked mentally and spiral into depression, just as I am not saying that a spiritually strong person can not be attacked mentally in non-spiritual areas. It sounds like no one can win this battle. Fortunately God has made provision for us. First of all, realize that you can win, and you will win if you use what God has provided for you. Secondly, you can turn this whole thing around on Satan and use this battle to get closer to God. It can get you on the right path if you weren't really on it. It can give you a huge incentive to get deeply into God's Word and, find the Way, the Truth and the Life which is Jesus Christ. Scriptures will suddenly "pop out" and give you real answers to your real questions. In fact, in my own case the Lord revealed to me that this was the only way to keep me from being eternally lost. I have no regret for the pain I went through. I embrace it. It really is a choice, too. You can give up and have nothing to do with God and His Word; or you can struggle, fight, fall down, get up and overcome the depression by God's healing power and His Word. Depression can make or break a new Christian or a person that thought about pursuing Christ, but turned to drugs, alcohol and pleasure to mask the pain.

There should be no shame and definitely no condemnation from fellow Christians. And fellow Christians should not, and I say emphatically, <u>not</u> discourage a Christian brother or sister from seeking professional and medical help. A depressed person may need the medical treatment (which is really God's healing) before a spiritual journey can begin. This is my opinion, and it was true for me. I know that God can do a miracle suddenly or He can do it over many years which is how He worked mine; and I'm glad He did, because I learned a great deal.

You, who are reading this book, will ultimately win because you will win the spiritual battle. It's all in The Book. Eternal life is the free gift offered to you if you accept Christ as your Savior. Once you trust Him, you will find that He has the answers for all of your questions and an anchor for your life when you go through the storms. He gives me the peace that passes all understanding. He makes you and I new creations. How awesome is that! You leave the old creation behind; in fact it doesn't exist anymore. You can remember events, but the memory becomes dimmer and dimmer as time goes on.

Don't get into a mental battle with Satan. Use scripture against Him just as Jesus did when He was in the desert being tempted by him. None of us know all there is to know in the Bible, but use scripture that you know and ask for the Holy Spirit's guidance. Lean not on your own understanding. That is how you win battles, with the Word of God. Don't become frustrated if God just doesn't reveal the meaning of a particular verse the first time you read it. He will reveal the meaning to you when you need it. Answers will come but in God's timing. Be content with what God reveals to you. It is sufficient.

There are cautions and warnings in the Bible concerning arguments and mental struggles or mental struggles over unimportant things. Foolish discussions will cause you a lot of pain. Take Jesus at His Word. Worry ends where Faith begins.[1]

"And I have been chosen – this is the absolute truth – as God's minister and missionary to teach this truth to the Gentiles, and to show them God's plan of salvation through faith"[2] 1 Timothy 2:7

"For you must teach others those things you and many others have heard me speak about. Teach these great truths to trustworthy men who will in turn pass them on to others. Know what His Word says and means"

"Steer clear of foolish discussions which lead people into the sin of anger with each other."[3]

2 Timothy 1:2 2 Timothy 2:15

Why are these passages important to us? God knows how messed up we can get with depression, imaginations and feelings of hopelessness. I hope when you finish with this book you can say, "Okay, I get it. God gave us His Word, and His Word says we are guaranteed to win if we accept Christ as our Savior." There is a verse of scripture for every human need. Believe me, I know. You will find yours if you look.

Among some of the good things that come out of depression is the ability to help others suffering from depression. You're able to look back at where you were, and relate to them that you made it and that you're fine. They need to hear that and to get help soon, the sooner the better before it get's really dangerous. It helped me to be able to say to myself that, okay this why I had to go through this because God gave me a very special task, and it is to help those who have no idea of how they got into the shape they're in, how they're going to endure it, or how they're going to get out of it. I wish I had been able to talk to someone when it happened to me. It was such a blessing when my doctor put me at such ease and let me know that millions of people are diagnosed with this every year. He said he has told many of his patients about me, that I'm a Christian, and that their spirits were lifted when they were told of my circumstances – chemical imbalance. That really made me feel good.

"And that from a child thou hast known the holy scriptures, which were able to make thee wise unto salvation through faith which is in Christ Jesus"[4]

2 Timothy 3:15

I know that Satan attacked me in my mind throughout my 30 year struggle, but through it all, when I took Jesus at His Word, worry ended and Faith began. Not one of us can please God without faith. The Bible says that the man who finds life will find it through trusting God. Through the years, I would be so desperate for an answer and find that if I just trusted what Jesus said, I wouldn't have a problem. In the book of Revelation it says:

"Him that overcometh will I make a pillar in the temple of my God"[5]

Revelation 3:12

It's very tough to overcome many of the predicaments we find ourselves in, but when we do, what exhilaration. And the more you overcome the more confidence you get and the more faith you use. We grow steadily and even though he knows the pain we feel, He nods approvingly. He sees Satan fall like lightning.

Many times, in order to overcome we must

have an eternal perspective. For the non-believer, the perspective is limited to the things of this earth, but for the Christians and for those seeking answers to life's questions, knowing that we are eternal beings gives us the eternal perspective we need. After all, life on this earth is very short and can end on any given day.

Although it's taken me many years to get this eternal perspective, it has given me a very peaceful frame of mind and instead of thinking of myself as a victim, I see myself as a useful tool for God. As long as I'm doing the will of God, which for me is being a good husband, a good father, grandfather, uncle and neighbor, and fitting into His will, that is sufficient.

This writing that I'm doing now for my neighbors and friends is part of God's will for me.

Chapter 20

Nothing is impossible

Along the same lines as an eternal perspective is the realization that nothing is impossible with God. This is true for our natural or physical being, but even more importantly in our supernatural (spiritual), mental and emotional well-being. Sometimes you may feel like you're in a hopeless situation or condition, but you're not. God has provided you with healing power. You really need to be free from your depression. There are 7 good reasons why you need your joy:

1. It keeps you healthy.
2. It will help your commitments.
3. It keeps your strength.
4. Joy is where your faith is located.
5. It draws God's presence.
6. It brings deliverance.
7. Joy opens up your destiny.[1]

At one time in my life, I thought I was going to have to live in a state of depression for the rest of my life. I was determined to do it, but the longer I went without treatment, the more I realized I could not do it. I thought I was going to lose my wife. We didn't have any kids at the time. You may feel that way too. If you do, get help immediately. The longer you go without treatment, the longer it will take to come out of your condition. Don't listen to the voices that are preventing you from going to get help. Don't worry about what family members will think. That's one thing that held me back, I didn't want every one to know how weak I was and that I was having a breakdown. They don't need to know anyway, do they? But if they know, big deal.

Time helps us heal. What is 70 or 80 years compared to eternity? The place that we're broken is healed and is a fading memory. We may never forget it, but when it does come to mind, we will be reminded of God's grace and mercy. If part of the problem is a forgiveness issue we must forgive ourselves, because God certainly has. If we must forgive someone that has hurt us, we must do it. God forgave us.

"Leave it to me and I will lead you home." The Holy Spirit spoke that to me in the mid 1980's.

To me Matthew 7:7-11 is the greatest. This scripture has never let me down, and I know it never will. I have defeated Satan with it countless upon countless times. God loves me so much, Jesus loves me so much and the Holy Spirit loves me so much. I really realize how much God loves me, and everyone for that matter. It's a gift to me but others as well and I know that millions of others around the world and through the years have held onto these verses as well. Thank you God. He knew that I needed these words spoken by Jesus, and whether I live for another 20 years or another 20 days, I will believe these scriptures and all scriptures. I will trust Jesus as I have all of these years and I will keep these words in my heart. I praise God for the precious blood that He shed on Calvary for my sins to be forgiven and I praise God for the Words Jesus spoke.

Who else but God could give eternal life?

Since everything the prophets said was true, how much more then is everything Jesus said true?

Something very key to reading and understanding the scriptures is this scripture. 2 Timothy 3:16 says, "All scripture is given by inspiration of God and is profitable for doctrine, for reproof, for correction, for instructions in righteousness." The Living translation: "The whole Bible was given to us by inspiration from God and is useful to teach us what is true and to make us realize what is wrong in our lives; it straightens us out and helps us do what is right."[2]

"When I was with you before you don't

remember me telling you that everything written about me by Moses and the prophets and in the Psalms must all come true?"[3]

Luke 24:44

Clearly to me, a truth about God's Word is that everything in God's Word is written by His inspiration and helps us in our daily lives. (Keep that in mind when you read books of history or prose.) There is something in there that is profitable for us and inspired by God. The Bible is God's Book of instructions. If you don't follow the instructions, you can get into trouble.

Also clearly to me, Jesus Who is the Word made Flesh and Who is the Truth stated that what the prophets and Moses said about Him must come true. And Jesus is greater than the prophets, so whatever He said, you can count on it to be true.

If you're like me, there will be times in your life when you will need a Word to count on. Look to the Words Jesus spoke.

I wrote this in 1993 and it really just sums up the way I feel about the Words Jesus spoke.

Simple Words

Simple Words, Words of Faith

Overcoming, claiming victory time and again

Always claiming victory time and again
Always claiming victory, as though losing could not be

Many though reject the simple words
Of the Man of Sorrows, allowing victory to slip away
As though they were never in sight
Demons dance in delirious glee
Each time the step of faith is not taken

Some would that the words had more
of man's influence, spilling from the
intellects and passion of a statesman or a
War hero, or perhaps an entertainer
Then words would be absorbed and nurtured
For a lifetime as a brilliant product to treasure

His Ways are not ours, our ways are not His
Are we to question our Creator?
Are we to reject so callously the Truth?
Simple Words, Words of Truth

Trusting is like breathing to me now and I wrote this on November 1993:

Trusting

Trusting in God's promise is something
That I could not do without. It is good
That here is something that anyone can have.
Trusting in God's promises is so precious that
It is priceless. One cannot buy it, and yet
Anyone can have it.

You are to be praised, for making
Your promises available to everyone.

I'll never forget Your promise Lord,
For they are emblazoned on my heart.
Your Words of Truth are forever mine.

Help me Lord to understand more.
There is so much to be learned from your
Precious Word. I have learned how to live
From studying your Word.

You are to be praised, Lord for making
Your promises available to everyone.

In the past and in the present Your Word
Has revived me from discouragement. I know
They will in the future if needed.
Open my eyes Lord so that I may know more.

Trusting in Your promises is far more
Profitable than making money or gaining fame.
Trusting in Your promises renewed my life, for this
Is Your promise – to save me.

Your promises are my only sure things
Man's promises can fail. Your promises
Remain faithful always. They refresh me
When I am sorely in need.

I wonder why everyone doesn't trust in Your
promises
Isn't eternal life there? Don't all things
Of the world evaporate?

There was a time when I thought
You were only to be feared.
That caused me to seek the Truth.
I found it, Your Word.
Now I have Your promises, and a healthy fear of You
Lord, my God.

I know I would have despaired and perished
Had it not been for Your promises.
I will never lay them aside, because
You have used them to restore my
Joy and health.

Though the world fall around me,
I will quietly keep my mind on Your promises.

Nothing is perfect except for You and Your Words
And You have given Your Words and so they are perfect.
Oh how I love them and how I love You.
I think about them a lot
Not as much as I should.

Your Words have enabled me to understand much
I see suffering in the world as it goes through
Its death throes. I think,
If only everyone were to listen to Your promises.
That is not to be though, because of forces
Of evil that we cannot see, but manifest
Themselves in the things that we can.

Your Words are so wonderful
No wonder I love them.
As Your plan unfolds, it is easy to see
That even the simple can understand it.

I am happy to include myself in that group
...The simple. For a child has simple faith
And he trusts perfectly, and to such as these
All is given.

I am praying and telling you how much I love You
You know this already of course.

As I meditate on your promises, I know that
You are very, very near. You are within me.
You are forever to be praised, for You have
Made Your promises available to everyone.

Every good and perfect gift is coming down from the Father of the heavenly lights, who does not change like shifting shadows. He chose to give us birth through the Word of Truth that we may be a kind of first fruits of all He created. I've come to know that one precious gift God gave us is the miracle of medication. I've written a lot about this already, but there needs to be an emphasis on this subject. There are those that would say, "You don't have any faith if you see doctors and take medication for depression." So much of the world was made for man to discover. God wanted the world to be interesting. There are always things to be discovered in the fields of astronomy, physics, engineering and medicine to name just a few.

Think for a moment that someone finds a cure for cancer. Would many people reject it and say that people who use it don't have any faith? Sadly some would. But the majority of us have no problem taking medication for diabetes, cholesterol, infections, ulcers, polio, measles, mumps and the list could go on and on. The typical comment you get is, “Get a hold of yourself”, “snap out of it” or “you’ll get over it.” If you’re suffering from clinical depression, you’re not going to “snap out of it”, and you can’t “get over it” and you cannot “get a hold of your self”. Listen, you can’t snap out of diabetes, heart disease or kidney disease. So why the double standard? One reason, I suppose is that people associate depression with weakness, which couldn’t be farther from the truth. Remember some of the folks mentioned earlier that suffered with depression? Were they weak?

I wrote this in November of 1999. “My life is becoming less and less self-centered and I’m interested in others. Things of the world are getting less and less important and the things of God are everything to me. I’m happier and I just enjoy the simpler things in life. I have a wonderful wife sons and family. My possessions are only good to be given away and to brighten someone else’s life. Kids are great and I enjoy pointing them to Christ.”

CHAPTER 21

A RENOVATION PROJECT

I know a place is being prepared for me in heaven and it's perfect, not like earthly houses, especially my house.

Isaiah 40:6-8. Isaiah compared life to a wildflower that quickly wilts and fades.[1] We need to keep this in mind with all of our dealings, emotions, and decision-making. We need to keep an eternal perspective.

Jeremiah 3:29, 30. He said, "People shall no longer quote this proverb – 'Children pay for their father's sins', for everyone shall die for their own sins."[2] This scripture meant a lot to me , because if Jeremiah could prophecy that people would no longer quote a proverb, then how much more then could Jesus change the old Law. A good example of this is when Jesus said that Moses' law said that a man could get rid of his wife by writing a letter of dismissal, but Jesus said that divorce was wrong and that it caused adultery. He said that God allowed this because of the stubbornness of the Israelites. Therefore, whatever Jesus said is the absolute Truth and should be considered clarification of any scriptures that you don't understand. Or if you hear something from the pulpit or from friends that seem confusing to you, look to what Jesus said.

And again, "Am I not everywhere in all of heaven and earth?"[3] Jeremiah 23:24. (Just in case you're wondering if God is everywhere.)

And then Jeremiah 17:7…"But blessed is the man who trusts in the Lord and has made the Lord his hope and confidence."[4] This scripture was one of the many that helped me trust in the Lord completely. It caused me to write boldly in my journal, "Take Jesus at His Word" 10/99

If anyone is struggling with depression and the enemy is seeking to convince them that the Word was only for the disciples or for people of that time, consider the scripture:

"And I tell you this in solemn truth that wherever the Good News is preached throughout the world, this woman's deed will be remembered and praised."[5]

Mark 14:8

Besides the obvious documentation of what this woman did, the Holy Spirit revealed a truth to me. The good News is being preached throughout the world today and has been since Jesus spoke these words. So the Good News as stated by Jesus is for everyone who has lived since the Words were spoken. They were intended for whoever heard it. The Good News is for whoever is present when the Good News is preached. Since the Good News is for everyone everywhere, the whole Word is for us all. Praise God.

Since the Good News is for everyone everywhere, so many scriptures started jumping out at me and I had to write them down.

"All that believe the Good News about Christ will be brought into heaven..."[6]

Romans 1:16, 17

"This is accomplished from beginning to end by faith. The man who finds life will find it through trusting God..."[7]

"God's Word will always prove true and right, no matter who questions them."[8]

Romans 3:4

"If we trust in Jesus Christ, Who in His kindness freely takes away our sins..."[9]

Romans 3:24

"He used Christ's blood and our faith as a means of saving us from His wrath."[10]

Romans 3:25

"He does it on the basis of their trust in Jesus who took away their sins."[11]

Romans 3:26

"It is based on what Christ has done and our faith in Him. So it is that we are saved by faith in Christ."[12]

Romans 3:27

"The only condition is that you freely believe in the Truth, standing on it steadfast and firm, strong in the Lord, convinced of the Good News that Jesus died for you."[13]

Colossians 1:23

This little poem says a lot about having faith in Christ instead of worrying. It meant a lot to me. Maybe it will to you.

I'll trust my all to God alone

Whose Word is Truth and Light.

I'd rather walk by Faith with Him

Than go alone by sight.

My mind really needed to be renewed. The more I read the Bible the more I realized this. Yes I had a clinical problem, but after all of that was stabilized; I really needed a renewing of my mind. "It's a bit like finding that you have a leaky roof and you fix the leak, but then you spend a lot of time fixing the water damage. Or like finding that you have a termite problem. You kill all the termites and set up a maintenance program to keep them controlled, but then you spend a long time repairing all of the termite damage in your floor, walls and roof."[14]

Phase I of my renovation project was chemical imbalance (physical) and emotional. Having it was a nightmare and not knowing where it would lead to or not knowing what I was going to do was almost worse, the not-knowing factor. I felt weak and spineless and not like a man at all. Yet looking back, it was the toughest thing I ever did to cling to what I had and hold onto Barbara. In a strange sense it sharpened my survival instincts and will to live. It actually was the destruction of my life as I knew it and was living it, so that something much better could be laid as a foundation for my life. I knew not who or what it was at the time.

We have talked at length about the different medications there are today for depression. No matter which one is prescribed, accept whatever it is as the method God has in place to get you back to normalcy. Remember that it could take three to six months to get there, but you will start to feel better in four to five weeks. You will see the difference. Your anti-depressants are not happy pills. They work by making you want to feel better; it's hard work but your compulsive thoughts will begin to ease up and the intense emotional pain will ease up.

You will have the strength to face the thoughts that were never resolved, dealt with or completed. There will be days that you feel as though you took two steps backward and one step forward, but stick to the task. Know that this is a temporary issue, and the beginning of a life-changing and supremely worthy renovation project. Eventually you will want to renew your mind, think differently and put the past behind you. That's where God comes in and that was the beginning of Phase II of my renovation project. I pray that it's yours too.

In *Where the Roots Reach for Water,* Jeffery Smith describes his own renovation project. Here are some excellent quotes from that book:

"I had conquered nothing, mastered nothing, and transcended nothing. I had simply settled into something that had been waiting for me-who knows how long?-and made the descent it seemed to require.

In that descent I had lost all sense of myself; but as that alienation persisted, I'd felt replacing my small self a sustaining kinship with other people alive and long dead. And I'd been given a life unimaginable to that former self: now I was in love, and I was trying to live with faith in something unseen, and I was restored to my family. Perhaps there is no unity without mystery; perhaps I had to become utterly disoriented before I could find and inhabit the landscapes that claimed me, my native places.

This is what melancholia taught me: in some landscapes we see more plainly from beneath the earth…in an arid and barren place you must splay the roots broad and deep and let them take some saturnine burrowing, you must trust them to trawl through the hardpan and clay that will scarcely nourish them, and find their way to water…all this oneness begins in those roots, and those roots take shape from their grasp; and that grasp is the shape of faith, the root tunneling blind through he closed dark earth in its ever uncertain-but still unceasing-reach: for water."

CHAPTER 22

A NEW THING

"Remember ye not the former things neither consider the things of old. Behold I will do a new thing, now it shall spring forth, shall ye not know it? I will even make a way in the wilderness, and rivers in the desert."[1]

Isaiah 43:18, 19

He tells us over and over again, a line at a time, and in such simple words.

Isaiah 28:10, 13

God wants us to see a bigger picture. Phase II of my Renovation project began when I realized that God can and will renew your mind. "Renovation projects usually require that things get a little worse before they get better. Your soul is where your mind is. It's the control center. If it get's busted, out of whack or in need of an overhaul, you are broken, you need fixing. God is the only mechanic that can work on your soul. How does He do it?"[2]

READ WHAT JESUS SAID AND BELIEVE IT. This will be the start of a long process, but a permanent result. It doesn't have to be a long project, but in my case it was. I was a tough nut to crack. Read Matthew, Mark, Luke and John. They're in the Bible at the beginning of the New Testament. Read Matthew 7:7-11, that's a good place to start.

"There are some things that we must see to walk in faith and to have peace of mind.

1. The basis of every struggle is fear.
2. Locate the things that are feeding the fear and remove them.
3. The enemy's plan is to attack your thought life with fear.
4. Pain is a highly concentrated thought."[3]

God is greater than we can imagine. His ways are not our ways. His Words were given to Jesus to speak to us. They are all true. He knows what our needs are as humans, and His Words meet every human need. I needed peace of mind and an unwavering faith. What I had was all of the above: fear, things feeding the fear, a messed-up thought life and intense emotional pain.

God wants us to be over comers. And to be over comers, we have to have something to overcome, right? This is another important perspective. The suffering from depression or other emotional pain is worth it.

Consider the words of Peter in 1 Peter 1:7: "These trials are only to test your faith, to see whether or not it is strong and pure. It is being tested as fire tests gold and purifies it – and your faith is far more precious to God than mere gold. So if your faith remains strong after being tested in the test tube of fiery trials, it will bring you much praise and glory and honor on the day of His return."[4]

Verse 9 – "And the further reward for trusting Him will be the salvation of your souls."[5]

1 Peter 4:12 "Dear friends don't be bewildered or surprised when you go through fiery trials ahead, for this no strange unusual thing that is going to happen to you. Instead be really glad – because these trials will make you partners with Christ in His suffering, and afterwards you will have the wonderful joy of sharing His glory in that coming day, when it will be displayed."[6]

1 Peter 5:6 "If you will humble yourselves under the mighty hand of God, in His good time He will lift you up. Let Him have all your worries and cares, for He is always thinking about you and watching everything that concerns you. Verse 10 – After you have suffered a little while, our God who is full of kindness through Christ, will give you His eternal glory. He will personally lift you up, and set

you firmly in place, and make you stronger than ever. To Him be all power over all things, forever and ever. Amen."[7]

Through all these verses I saw that my suffering was not some kind of weird, unusual thing and that many people will suffer. Depression is definitely suffering. And I saw that God cares about our suffering but that He will lift us up in His good time, and that we will eventually share in His eternal glory through Christ, the Word made Flesh.

At one time, I thought that all my depression, the fear and the obsessive thoughts were all about me and a flaw, an internal flaw that I thought was my fault. I blamed myself for being a weak man. But I got a significant breakthrough in this destructive thinking through this next verse and many, many others in scriptures that reveal the real culprit in all of these mental and spiritual struggles.

1 Peter 5:8 "Be careful – watch out for attacks from Satan, your great enemy. He prowls around like a hungry, roaring lion, looking for victims to tear apart. Stand firm when he attacks. Trust the Lord and remember that other Christians all around the world are going through these same sufferings too."[8]

Satan assaults our mind. That's how he can best defeat us, with depression, fear, doubt, worries and anxiety. He is the father of lies. Jesus is the Way, the Truth and the Life. The way to defeat Satan is through the Word of God and especially what His Son Jesus said.

When Satan was tempting Jesus with all kinds of suggestions, Jesus replied, "No! For the Scriptures tell us that bread won't feed men's' souls, obedience to the Word of God is what we need." And again, It also says not to put he your God to a foolish test." And again, "Get out of here Satan. The Scriptures say, "Worship only the Lord God. Obey Him."[9]

Matthew 4:4-10

So Jesus used scripture to defeat Satan's attempt to assault His mind. This became my defensive and offensive plan to regain complete control of my mind and it really is the only plan that works. But again, if you have a chemical imbalance, you can't think straight, please see your doctor.

God didn't make us with flaws; sin brought all kinds of suffering into the world. Some may argue that God made us, so isn't it His fault that we have chemical imbalances that cause depression? Well with that argument, you arrive at God being the cause of all sickness, mental and physical, from depression to Alzheimer's to birth defects to cancer.

No, God created Adam and Eve and a Garden of Eden and because of Adam's sin after being tempted by Satan, sickness and death entered our lives. God gave Adam a free will as He does all of us. He allowed the choices to be made. Now God is all-powerful so He could, of course stop all of the pain and suffering, but instead He uses it to ultimately defeat Satan.

Jesus did that on the cross. Now we can use our own "cross" of depression to defeat Satan as well. My depression brought me to the beginning of a long journey to an abundant life here and to eternal life beginning here and lasting forever in heaven.

Although clinical depression is a physical condition, something usually triggers it. Many times this "something" is past thoughts or experiences.

1 Thessalonians 5:23 says that we are comprised of spirit, soul and body.[10] The soul is a place of storage, leading and filtering so it contributes much to our well-being and our misery. My own past thoughts were thoughts of sins that I had committed and some things that I had not done, but Satan had caused me to imagine that I had done things because of my obsessions. Boy did I ever need mind renewal. Today when I look back, I'm amazed at how the mind works and how under the right mental state combined with fragments of

unrelated memories and fear, I could be that confused and tormented. Satan, your enemy and my enemy, is an expert at these things.

Why do past thoughts rise up? As usual, God takes what the enemy tries to harm us with and uses it for our good.

1. It is God wanting us to see our wrong dependencies.
2. It is God who is wanting us to see the Truth.
3. It is the thought itself because it was never resolved, dealt with or completed."[11]

God doesn't want us to have messed-up minds and messed-up lives. Jesus came to give us abundant life, to bring healing to our lives. 1 Corinthians 2:16 says that we have the mind of Christ.[12]

"Avoid the trap of looking back – unless it's to recall a lesson learned or to glory in what God has accomplished. For those whose lives are centered in Christ, the best days are yet to come. To live in the past is to miss today's opportunities and tomorrow's blessings."[13]

A lot of folks get hung up on doing things the way they've always been done, presumably because they feel comfortable with the familiar ways. An example of this is the way that we praise, the way we worship and the way that we sing. I was brought up on the Catholic hymns and songs, now I also enjoy the faster paced music of today, in today's language. It's not that I don't enjoy the older songs to a degree; it's just that I have been moved to tears by the words of the newer songs and I've seen young people moved to tears and their lives changed by some of the Christian rock bands' music that a lot of young people listen to today. I myself have been to concerts and have been moved and seen hundreds of young people come to Christ at these concerts. There are many that would scoff at this as "not the real thing". But God is not to be put in a box.

The same is true for physical healing. Anti depressant medication did not exist even 70 years ago, but it does now and it eases people's suffering and allows them to think clearly and see their way clear out of depression. Could that be a bad thing? I don't think Jesus would think so. He was all for easing the sufferings of people, and healed people of all sorts of afflictions and cast out demons. He had compassion for people because they were like sheep without a shepherd.

An anonymous author wrote, "Hope is the ability to hear the melody of the future. Faith is the courage to dance to its tune today."

Chapter 23

Reasonings and Doubt

I very much dislike these words. They were such a part of my life for so long. How different now, replaced with faith and assurance.

Dr. Martyn Lloyd Jones said in one of his sermons: When you are puzzled and perplexed, the thing to do is to try and find something of which you are certain, and then take your stand on it.

"For the Kingdom of God belongs to men who have hearts as trusting as these little children's. And anyone who doesn't have their kind of faith will never get into the Kingdom's gates".[1]

Luke 18:17

Jesus also said that He has hidden things from the wise and revealed it to babes. For many years, I didn't "feel" saved, and I reasoned and reasoned and reasoned. And I realize that there was a purpose to all of it. God told me one time though, "Would a little child struggle this much? No, he would say, 'Well Jesus said we could ask God for stuff and He would give us what we ask for'. The child would ask God for forgiveness and know that he had it, he'd ask for eternal life and know that he had it and ask for guidance and know that he had it." So God said, "Virgil, accept all of these things like a child."

Trust the little red words (what Jesus said) and trust the Holy Spirit.

Brothers, listen! In this man Jesus there is forgiveness for your sins. Everyone who trusts in him is freed from all guilt and declared righteous – something the Jewish law could never do. Oh be careful! Don't let the prophets words apply to you. For they said, "Look and perish you despisers of the Truth, for I am doing something in your day – something you won't believe when it is announced".[2]

This scripture should help us embrace the Truth. I know that when you're in a depressed state of mind, it's difficult to accept good news. (Oh that's too good to be true, that just couldn't be). But the Word is true, Jesus is the Word made Flesh and He is the Way the Truth and the Life. Please accept the Truth today. God is tenderly waiting for you to do just that. God's Word is greater than your mind and what you think and greater than your emotions and how they feel.

Faith is not a sense, a sight or a reason, but taking God at His Word. It says in Romans that God will not break His promises. "Though everyone else in the world is a liar, God is not. Do you remember what the Book of psalms says about this? That

God's words will always prove true and right, no matter who questions them."[3]

Romans 3:3, 4

"The queen of Sheba shall rise against this nation in the Judgment, and condemn it; for she came from a distant land to hear the Wisdom of Solomon; and now a greater than Solomon is here – and you refuse to believe him."[4]

Matthew 12:42

Once again Jesus spoke about doubt in Matthew when he was giving John the Baptist's disciples a message for John who was in jail. John had sent his disciples to see Jesus and ask Him if He was really the Messiah, or should they keep looking.

"Then give him this message, 'Blessed are those who don't doubt me'."[5]

Matthew 11:2-6

Was Jesus upset with John? No, he told the crowds that of all men ever born, none shone more brightly than John.

You know it really doesn't take a lot of faith to change your life. Why is it that we take just about everything that scientists say as the truth and don't give it a thought – and they're mere men. Jesus spoke about how the tiniest faith could work .

"For if you had faith even as small as a mustard seed you could say to this mountain, 'Move!' and it would go far away, Nothing would be impossible."[6]

Matthew 18:20

Whatever your mountain is, it can be moved and cast into the sea. Mine was depression, and it seemed like an obstacle impossible to move and have a normal life. If it's depression, you can and will get to the bottom of its cause and beat it down, if you ask for God's help and have faith. He cares about you.

"Be not afraid, only believe."[7]

Mark 6:36

That's pretty straightforward. Jesus said that right before he brought Jairus' daughter back to life.

"Anything is possible if you have faith"[8]

Mark 9:23

Jesus asked Bartimaeus, "What do you want me to do for you?" Bartimaeus answered, "O Teacher, I want to see!" Jesus promptly said, "Alright it's done. Your faith has healed you."[9]

Mark 10:51, 52

Where do these reasonings and doubt come from? Where else? The devil is the father of lies and he has a strategy. He's not in any kind of hurry and he knows that the devices that work the best are those that are subtle and are unleashed over a period of time. Thoughts, doubts, reasonings and theories are how he did it with me after the chemical imbalance made me so vulnerable. That's the other thing about the enemy, he's vicious and without mercy. He's observed us for centuries and he knows what works. What he used against me and what he's used against you is nothing new, he's utilized these strategies on untold numbers of others. The enemy will come in through the front door, window, back door or the roof but he will find a way to get in so you have to be prepared to throw him out.

The doubts will cause instability in your life, and will keep you ignorant of your power and authority in Jesus. There is a pureness of God's Word, in which every verse has a purpose, and many times we don't know that purpose. One of them though is to defeat the enemy. To overcome these assaults, we must use the only weapons that work, the Word, revelation given by the Holy Spirit and prayer. The enemy will wave something in front of you and say don't take this road, it will take faith. Believing what He said is more real than what you see. Put faith in your equation; the Bible says that we will find life by trusting God.

CHAPTER 24

PSALM 73

This psalm has taught me that life is filled with painful and perplexing problems which at times cause us to cry out: "Lord why don't you intervene?" Yet just about as our feet are about to slide out from under us something always comes to us to use – an idea or thought which if we hold onto it causes us to halt our downward progress. We find that if we act responsibly and do what is right even though we don't feel like it, we will experience inward change.

But it isn't God's purpose to bring a little change – He desires to bring about a lot of change. How does He achieve this? He does it by bringing us into His presence and revealing to us His Word. There we discover that our greatest problems are not the ones on the outside of us, but those on the inside of us – our perspectives are wrong. Real changes come about not when our feelings are soothed out, but when our thinking is changed. Changed thinking leads to changed desires. When our perspectives are controlled by the Word, rather than by the world, then we will experience inner peace. The psalmist resolved to draw near to God and stay close to Him so that he could see life steadily, and see it whole..

Everyone will be able to understand the struggle of the writer of Psalm 73: We start off with a positive faith in God's goodness and then something happens which causes us to be plagued with doubts. The problem is how to get back to where we were. That's what the psalmist does in this psalm – he shows us how to get back to the place where the soul finds its peace.

We should not forget that the strongest convictions are born in the throes of doubt. Doubts may discourage but they need not demoralize you. It's not what happens to you, but what you make of it that matters.

Selwyn Hughes on Psalm 73

I particularly like verses 22 through 28 of Psalm 73:

"I saw myself so stupid and ignorant; I must seem like an animal to you, O God. But even so you love me! You are holding my right hand! You will keep on guiding me all my life with your wisdom and counsel; and afterwards receive me into the glories of heaven! (I really like that part). Whom have I in heaven but you? My health fails; my spirits droop, yet God remains! He is the strength of my heart; He is mine forever!

But those refusing to worship God will perish, for he destroys those serving other gods.

But as for me I get as close to Him as I possibly can! I have chosen Him and I will tell everyone about the wonderful ways he rescues me.

CHAPTER 25

YOUR SPOUSE

If it were not for my wife Barbara, God's precious gift to me, my chances of surviving the depression would have been slim to none. She took her wedding vows seriously and stood by me, stayed with me and loved me. I can imagine how hard it was to be married to a man as depressed as I was. She had to see the long face going to work and the same long face when I came home. She knew that I had to put on a good "front" whenever we were with other people and pretend that everything was normal, and then watch me collapse into a chair when I got home. There was no planning for the future, there was no fun. Each day she would have hope that I would come out of it and would encourage me. She is the main reason that I was determined to come out of it. My love for her and her love for me made a huge difference. Barbara had to be the strong one in the marriage for awhile til I got back on my feet.

Possibly if you go through a period of depression in the future or if you are presently going through one, your spouse may not be quite so understanding and this not surprising. Many people do not understand the causes of depression, because up until a few years ago you didn't hear very much about it. No one liked to talk about it especially the sufferer or their family.

If you have not chosen a spouse yet but want to, it is so important to choose a spiritually mature, bible-believing Christian. Or at least to choose one that has started the journey. And on top of that it is important that the person be kind, loving, compassionate and understanding. This choice is the second most important choice you will ever make. This choice will impact how you weather life's storms.

Your spouse should know that depression is a medical condition many times accompanied by anxiety symptoms or co-existing anxiety disorder (for example, panic disorder). In the United States, over 14 million people suffer from depression any given year. Although depression can affect people of all ages, symptoms often appear for the first time in people in their mid 20s. As many as 25 percent of women suffer from depression, enough to seek treatment, at least once in their lifetime. In fact, nearly twice as many women as men suffer from depression every year.[1] But I think this disparity is a little smaller in reality, because a lot of depressed men never seek treatment. Through every phase of my recovery God worked through my "Sweetness", Barbara. Always praying for me with her prayer group buddies or in her own prayer time, always making sure I had plenty of my meds, always there encouraging me at times and other times reassuring me that I would get better. She was doing her part in God's plan to see to it that I arrived in that place under the wings of the Almighty, the only real source of peace that passes all understanding, which guards both heart and mind in Christ Jesus. (Phil. 4:7)[2]

One of the most important things she did was to keep the family moving along as close to some sense of normalcy as possible. The first wave of depression hit in 1973-1974, but I still had non-sensical issues that came up from 1975-1979; and then from 1980 -1984 I had spiritual issues that were disruptive. For awhile there, it was always something; it was always due to really defective thinking and obsessions about imaginary (but very real to me) problems. That's the nature of clinical depression; something finally triggers an episode and until I received medical treatment on a continual basis, I was going to be depressed about something. Barbara was always supportive, but did not allow me to just wallow in self pity. Our lives continued as normal as possible, as I grew and healed and learned how to cope with my depression and see it as an asset rather than a liability.

Barbara was a family person. She loved me and the boys and saw me become a more sensitive person with a real faith as I worked through all of the various hard times. I would pray for God to please help me to be a better husband and a better father, and you know what He did. God used Barbara in many ways to help answer that prayer. I give God all of the honor and glory for doing what He did in my life, but I know that God can use anyone and anything to accomplish His purposes.

One thing that she did was to continue to honor and respect me as her husband, which I know at times, was hard. But she was living by biblical principles, and because of her obedience, I was more able to become a better husband and father.

On December 18, 1984 I wrote, "Started out with a new life. I learned about a kind, loving, merciful God who forgives if only we ask. We don't have to do anything else – just change our lives. And in this new life, we don't have to worry about the future." On December 24, 1984 I wrote, "I learned that Satan has been responsible for all of my miseries and sufferings. I know that I'm going to heaven." I remember that day very well. We had just taken Jared and Joey to a special Children's' service at St. Phillip's Church. I came out and the Lord had spoken to me as we walked out of the service, very simple words but it indicated a very big change in my thinking and perspective. It was Barbara's idea to go to that service. Around the same time I wrote, "This entire episode was a test of your faith in which you fought a great battle against the enemy and you are victorious." That was a Word from the Lord. Then again, "This entire episode is now over with. All that is left is a painful memory and I will heal it." It took a while for that to sink in. I spent so many years wondering if I had done something to lose my salvation, but it was all a big deception. The enemy had studied me long enough and knew where my weaknesses were and as a result, knew just what buttons to push to try to destroy my life. The enemy is a trickster and he will try to deceive us with evil schemes.

Barbara wrote me the sweetest notes. Once for example she told me that she loved me and thanked me for a wonderful weekend, and that this family "owed" their wonderful weekends to me. She said that for a long time she has loved me, but here recently she loved my spirit too. She saw a change in me due to my spiritual self – in tune with the Holy Spirit. She thanked God for me and what He was doing in my life. That was over 20 years ago, but I still remember the encouragement that note gave me. I've saved that note and many others that she has given me. What an encouragement a spouse can be! I was having my problems, but God was making me a better husband and father.

I remember on one of our vacations to Disney World, maybe the 1983 trip, I really messed up. I should have listened to Barbara. We were at Epcot and I was really feeling down, but covering up well. At Germany, there were some performers/ entertainers that were pretty lively and I was clapping and making all sorts of noise. Barbara told me that I was drawing a bit too much attention to myself, and she was right. Little did I know but this little group of entertainers drew people from the crowd to participate; and as I was so lively, one of the young ladies came down and got me by the hand and pulled me up to the front. I had to put on a rubber "clown" nose and dance with an older lady that they also picked on. We danced and sang and generally made everybody laugh. Barbara and the boys got a laugh out of it, so that was worth it I guess.

I was miserable and nobody knew it. Outwardly I seemed perfectly fine. I knew that the skit would last but for a few minutes, and then I could go back to my family, so I was able to endure it. In the overall scheme of things, that's how I felt about my depression. I always believed that there would be a light to the end of this tunnel, and it was just around the corner. I knew that all of my obsessive thoughts were completely irrational, and all of this darkness would have to end.

Don't make the mistake of bailing out of your marriage if you're suffering from depression. I didn't make that mistake but a lot of people have. Leaving your marriage makes about as much sense as an attempted suicide. It doesn't solve a thing. Your spouse loves you and married you for the good times and the bad, that's what your vows said. They just want you to get better; they don't want you to bail on them. You need to get the help that is available. Marriages aren't trouble-free. Don't think that your marriage is the only one that has ever had this kind of stress in it. Try to see it as having that special person in your life, your soul mate, your life-long best friend, your spouse to help you through this difficult time. They really do want to, they just want you to do your part and try. Make the effort. Isn't it worth it? In a few months you'll be glad you did, and you and your spouse will love each other even more and have an even stronger marriage because you overcame this temporary crisis. If it turns out that this is a long-term chemical imbalance to deal with, it's okay; you can live a normal life. In fact you'll have an even better appreciation for life and will enjoy life even more; especially if you were just coasting along in life taking everything for granted.

CHAPTER 26

YOUR KIDS

Almost a year after my initial bout with depression, Barbara became pregnant with Jared our oldest son. Jared was a joy followed 25 months later by Joey another joy – and we were a family. As Joey would say later, "We are our family". My boys didn't know it at the time, but they were really helping me. The love that you feel for your wife and children, make you want to keep trying. When nothing else is going your way and you come home and have two rambunctious boys and a loving, supporting wife, your troubles sort of melt away, especially on weekends. Oh I still had bad times but my family was my complete anchor until I discovered the loving God that had been there for me all along.

Sometimes you have to tough it out for your wife and kids. That's always the case, but I'm talking about depression. You need to be there for them; you need to take care of yourself for their sake. There are so many good times to look forward to. Don't ever think about ending it all, it's just a permanent solution to a temporary problem. God never gives us more than we can handle. He always has a way out for us, a light at the end of the tunnel, if you will.

I remember Saturday afternoons after working in the yard all day coming in taking a shower piling up on the sofa bed with Barbara, Jared and Joey and watching Super Book and Flying House. These were two kids' animated shows that brought bible stories and principles to life and were tons of fun. I think the Lord blessed me with some very enjoyable times watching these shows with my family; they gave me some hope somehow that there could be better days ahead.

In mid 1980, I was really doing a lot better, but there were some feelings that I needed more. I realized that I wanted an even closer relationship with God, and I began seeking an active body of bible teaching and believing Christians at the same time. As my relationship with God grew and I noticed that I loved people more and wanted to associate with God's people. Barbara and I attended prayer groups, study groups and visited various churches. We landed at a Pentecostal Church and after a few years Barbara and I were doing Children's Church, and Jared and Joey helped us as teachers and puppeteers. This had been our hearts' desire for a long time. We developed many friendships there and although there were tough times, the experience of teaching the Word of God to kids was such a blessing.

It was one Sunday morning after we had first arrived at this church, that someone came into the church and said that there had been an accident involving a motorcycle on highway 17 right in front of our church. Without really knowing what I was doing I rushed out to the scene with another man. The scene was pretty chaotic, but also kind of quiet as a paramedic had already arrived and was working on the young man. The traffic was backed up, of course, and there was a small group of people gathered around some of which were laying there hands on the man and praying for him. I uncharacteristically put my hand on him and began to pray for his life. I noticed blood coming from his nose and ears, and the paramedic was saying, "We're losing him, we're losing him!" Then almost as soon as I put my hand on him, the paramedic said something like, I'm getting a pulse or His pressure is coming back up. God healed that man by the prayer of those people, but I think that God let his recovery begin when I put my hand on him to bless me, give me encouragement and let me know that He was with me.

I was also active in the Cub Scouts and Boy Scouts for a few years before the Children's Ministry which was unusual for me. There were camping trips, den and scout meetings, Pinewood Derby and Merit badges. Now the Pinewood Derby was interesting, in that the cars started out as a block of wood and the kids carved out the shape that they wanted. They then painted it and put on the wheels and prepared it for racing. Now the dads helped the boys, some a lot more than others. My boys' cars were always the ugliest; because I insisted that they do all of the painting. Some of the other kid's cars looked like they rolled out of a showroom.

Through the years sports was always a big part of our life. Baseball, football and soccer were Saturday morning mainstays. Many times the games were a pleasant escape from depression. Activities with Barbara and the boys were such a soothing balm for me and I didn't really want to do much of anything else. As I gradually felt better through the years and continued on being a family oriented dad, I remember feeling so grateful to God that I suffered from depression, if only that I started off right with my priorities. It was God then Barbara and the boys, then others and myself. Now I haven't always put others before myself, but I pretty much put God and family first. Now I'm definitely not saying that I think there is anything wrong with husbands and fathers doing stuff with others besides their families; just that I spent most of my time with my family and I'm glad that I did. I have no regrets

I think my countenance must have changed significantly. For example, my six year old niece, Kelly who would have nothing to do with me from the time she was born, climbed up on my knee without even being asked. Sometime later she asked me to give her some drawing tips. When she was about nine years old she told me that when she was real little, she was scared of me. So she must have seen a change in me. At least she lost her fear of me.

So I think it was about this time that I reached a new higher level of healing in my spirit. I loved family, I loved friends.

A quality that I gained gradually was mercy, and of course it made a difference. It wasn't that I was this real mean person that no one liked; it's just that at times I could have been a little more merciful. Selwyn Hughes summed it up very well, when he said, "Have you noticed how a person with the quality of mercy always seems to have good personal relationships? And when he or she has need of mercy from others it is instantly forthcoming, for as we give so shall we receive. And not only do they enjoy good personal relationships – they enjoy (other things being equal) good physical health. The right thing morally is the healthy thing physically."

On 11-18-99 I wrote:

My life is becoming less self-centered and I'm more interested in others. Things of this world are getting less and less important and the things of God are everything to me. I'm happier and happier and I just enjoy the good things of life. I have a wonderful wife, sons and family. My possessions are only good to be given away or to bring a little light into someone else's life. Kids are great and I enjoy pointing them to Christ. Everything is special. I know a place is being prepared for me in heaven, and it's perfect, not like an earthly home.

"Whoever finds his life will lose it, and whoever loses His life for my sake will find it."[1]

Matthew 10: 39

If you struggle with depression, the first thing you want to do is make sure you see your doctor and get the medication you need, realizing that this is healing that God has provided for you. Then deal with any issues head-on and resolve them. If that sounds like an over-simplification, it's because it is, but read the entire book. Next, really, really realize how blessed you are to have family; to have someone to love and someone to love you. Many of us treat other kids better than we do our own. Yes we have to discipline our kids and we can't just be their "buddy" all of the time, but you know what I mean. God has loaned us our kids and expects us to raise them right, but He wants us to love them unconditionally just as He loves us. If you do this, life will be better for them and better for you. They may be the best friends you have when you're older, but they get to make that choice and it's largely made on how well you loved them through their childhood and adolescence. Please don't expect to be absent during these years and expect everything to be wonderful with your kids when they're grown. My kids have been a source of joy for me when sometimes there wasn't a lot of joy to be found; and now that they're grown they are still a source of my joy. I'll always have them by my side. Love is found in being available to your kids as well. What greater joy than to be able to help them through tough times.

I will share this little story to show how not to love you kids. My boys wanted to go to a Christian concert about ninety miles away and I let them go but I didn't let them take the good car, the two year old Ford Explorer. No, instead I made them take the eight year old Oldsmobile that was not very dependable. Why did I do this? I don't know! Maybe I didn't want them messing up my new car? But since I wasn't as interested in their safety and security, they broke down, missed the concert and had to hitch a ride back to Charleston. I learned a lesson about what was more important and it was a turning point for me.

Now that I'm managing my depression and living a normal life it's wonderful to have them. If you have children, don't add to your struggles by losing them while you're going through struggles. That's why it's so important to get the professional and medical help that you need. If you won't do it because of some hang-up that you have about getting help then at least do it for the sake of your wife and kids. They don't understand your hang-ups they just want their dad. They expect you to be the best that you can be; they will admire you, when they're older for accepting God's provisions for your healing. They'll wonder why you didn't if you don't.

If depression strikes you when you and your kids are older, they may not "need" you like they did when you were a kid, but I'll bet they still want you to get help. And you know if they don't understand, or they're embarrassed, I'm sorry. You get the help you need anyway. If you're drowning and someone offers to throw you a life ring are you going to refuse because your kids are embarrassed that you can't swim? Come on.

I'm glad that today when I talk to my two grown sons about these times, they are amazed. They had no idea that I was going through these bouts with depression.

CHAPTER 27

OBSESSIVE THOUGHTS 2

When all you can think about is a real or imaginary sin, or any other thought for that matter, it is obsessive. A single-minded focus like this is an obsession. When a person is in this state, he or she may be unable to reflect rationally about this matter until the biochemistry causing such self-deprecation has been repaired.[1]

As I mentioned earlier there was a time in my life when I became obsessed with the notion that I had blasphemed the Holy Spirit, and I lived under a cloud of self-condemnation. I actually wasn't sure if I was really saved. Deep inside I did, but there was that nagging doubt. This problem is one of Satan's most utilized strategies in trying to hinder God's children from experiencing abundant life. This is what Selwyn Hughes, pastor and author has to say about it:

"What does it mean to blaspheme the Holy Spirit? In my view, it is willfully attributing to the Holy Spirit the filthiness of Satan. It is more than just a passing thought entering the mind; it is a continued stance of resistance which refuses to face the truth. And that sin is rarely committed. In my entire ministry I never met anyone that I thought had committed this sin. I have met many that believed they had done so, but close questioning revealed that it was not so much deliberate rebellion as obsessive thoughts – and that is really another problem.

The sin is so distinctive that anyone troubled about committing it shows, by the very fact that they are troubled, that they have not committed it. If they had the Holy Spirit would have departed and they wouldn't be troubled. Don't let Satan bully you into believing these obsessive thoughts are evidence that you have gone too far to be forgiven. If you want to be forgiven, your very wanting is a sign of the Spirit's presence in your life."

And the Holy Spirit revealed this very same thing to me, if you want to be forgiven, you can be, just ask. I had deep emotional problems because of my chemical imbalance. I was so messed up I believed just about every negative thought that came into my mind. Satan had me believing that I could have done things in my past that were really just obsessive thoughts I was having. You see I had just discovered the scripture on the blaspheming of the Holy Spirit. Satan put all kinds of thoughts in my mind that caused me to believe that my salvation was actually in question.

I've studied the scriptures for twenty-five years and I agree with Selwyn. If you want to be forgiven you can be, and it indicates the presence of the Holy Spirit in your life. If a person had committed a sin that couldn't be forgiven, I know that Satan would not bother that person's conscience for years and years because what would it gain Satan. But if you just think you did and were fearful, then Satan would love to keep you beaten down as long as he could.

God can use this kind of attack for good. In my case, I had to be totally broken and totally dependant on God and His Son, The Word made Flesh for every building block. I read the Bible exclusively for ten or fifteen years just so that I could avoid erroneous influence. After this period, I would occasionally read other books, but I was able to discern truth from opinion or error. During this period I was focused, the world had lost all of its appeal to me and I wanted to push on to my heavenly home with Jesus. I was able to let bondages be broken while I read God's Word and my mind became sensitive to God's signs and wonders like the dream I told you about earlier. I knew that dream and interpretation was from God and I knew that God noticed me and loved me. He cared about my comings and goings and predicaments.

"Nothing is perfect except for your words".[2]

Psalm 119:96

All of my mental suffering that I've gone through has caused me more than once to consider that my life could have been so much happier. My suffering brought me to Jesus, though, and after I was brought to Jesus, the enemy even attacked me more viciously. But I realized that if I had not suffered physically and mentally, if life had been more of a breeze, I would not be saved today. I have the attitude of Selwyn that unmerited suffering is going to come; it's a part of life. It's what we do with it that counts. Long ago sin unbalanced the universe and suffering is one of the inevitable results. If you deny that this is true then you deny reality, and the denial of reality is the denial of life. But God is able to turn the most vile and extreme suffering to good. All we have to do is accept this strange and wonderful fact. Character is formed in the furnace of affliction – no suffering, no character.

Accept suffering as a gift from God. I know that's easy to say, harder to do, but God knows the best way to achieve glory for you. Suffering is the best way to achieve glory for you. Suffering is His means to an end, if suffering is what you need; suffering is what He will allow. God isn't interested in our comfort; He is interested in our eternal security.

Selwyn Hughes said, "I can stand anything because I can use everything". Recognize that because you are finite, you will never be able to fully understand the ways of God. It was a wonderful moment in my life when I was delivered from the torment of trying to figure out the reasons that God behaves the way He does. After reading Isaiah 46:9-10, these thoughts hit me like a bolt from the blue: God is in control of the world. Don't try to grasp all the ramifications of this truth just accept it. I haven't spent a single moment trying to figure out why God does what He does. I accept His sovereignty without question – and I am all the better for it.

FACE THE FACT THAT GOD'S WAYS ARE UNSEARCHABLE AND UNFATHONABLE. THEN YOU WILL LIVE – REALLY LIVE.

CHAPTER 28

REALLY LIVING

You know, I was never going to really live the way I used to be, even before I had my first bout with depression. My pastor gave us a pretty good analogy. "I was like a glass of water with two inches of sediment (issues) in the bottom of it. That sediment will remain there until it's stirred up. God let's you get issues stirred up so He can skim it off or filter it out."[1] I was not going to get all of the issues addressed about truly living and I sure wasn't going to change myself, so God stirred me up. It took me a long time to understand what God was doing and why He was doing it. I decided that I had to step out of the mess I was in, and to do this I had to decide that I was in a mess. Acknowledging that you have a problem is hard, because it means it's going to take some work to resolve the problem.

Intense sincere prayer has to happen, and with it of course, a deep need that you know you are powerless to fill on your own. You're going to have some bumps in the road, but you've got to focus on God and not the bumps. There will be times when you don't think that you're making any progress and that you wonder if your medication is the right dosage. Satan will throw all kinds of cruel tricks at you, but you have to have the heart to go to war for your soul, your mind and your emotions. You have to be a man or woman of God willing to go to war for your spouse and your children.

Listen to the voice of the Lord. The Holy Spirit will lead you into all Truth. Praise God before during and after the victory that you will achieve. Continue to pray and worship God for what God is working in you. Be willing to obey a unique strategy. My strategy was to read and make mine the direct words of the Bible. I didn't rely on pastors, priests or other ministers to do my interpreting for me. I let the Holy Spirit do that. Additionally, I read no one else's interpretation of God's Word. I wanted what I received to be purely from the Holy Spirit. As my pastor says, "That's not even that crazy, but you have to keep your strategy even when people think you're crazy."

You'll have to sacrifice a lot. My family and I stopped seeing most movies that were produced. Just within the last ten years or so ago, technology produced what is called a TV Guardian, which removes any offensive words or phrases. There are some that think this is extreme and some that think that this is compromising. But this was and is part of my strategy. How could I tell my kids not to use bad language or not to see certain movies if they saw me do it?

You'll have to die to the opinions of your family and friends. I lost most of my old friends, but in doing so I built a stronger bond with Barbara, Jared and Joey. It's really kind of satisfying being a maverick and doing things your way rather than what seems right to everyone else.

Rejoice over your victory over enemies. It's alright to be happy when you experience a victory over some thing that you've struggled with for years. Build on each victory. That's so important to be able to look back and see from whence you came. That's why it's such a good idea to keep a journal. After every triumph receive it as a gift from the Lord and rest in His love and care.

Sometimes you can't modify what you have, you have to go out and find something new. That's the new creation that you need to become. Crossing the line from "what if", reasonings and calculations to faith is an absolutely necessary step. Why did it take me so long to get out of the "what if" mode? I had to reason out everything and it was just impossible. There aren't answers to everything attainable within ourselves. Why is there a God if not to have faith and trust in Him? Let God use your little bit of faith. To a child, a "little" looks like a lot. A little is all it takes; a speck is all it takes.

Set priorities.

Speak your faith. Faith is expectancy: "According to your faith will it be done to you."[2]

Matthew 9:29

You have to believe. I have found that whenever God speaks to us through His Word or in our inner man, we are not to reason, debate or ask ourselves if what He has said is logical. When God speaks we are not to rationalize.

You have to have a purpose. What is your purpose? Mine is simple. Love God with all my heart and my neighbor as myself. Be an overcomer, be a good husband, be a good dad and try to ease people's suffering. I want to shorten people's learning curve through depression and to help them find God.

Satan does not fight fair. Satan will exploit your poor decisions. He uses manipulation, domination and intimidation. So don't give him a foot hold. Keep your focus on your goal and not the diversions. You have many goals, but one goal is to be made whole and to let God use you. Focus on the solutions and not the setbacks; See the circumstance's potential and not the problem. Don't let the enemy drag you into depression.

I have God but not many friends, but that's okay. Jesus is my best friend, and God gave me

Barbara to be my best earthly friend. That sounds like a funny way to describe her, but you know what I mean. She is my soul mate who has stuck by me through the tough times.

Focus on your faith and not your failure. Faith is a potent thing. You get into the Kingdom by faith and you overcome evil by faith. Faith is what really frightens the enemy. The enemy is the accuser, who reminds us of our failures and past sins. The past sins don't even exist anymore, and we just learn from our failure we don't dwell on them. What good does that do? It's pointless. Each day is a new day. A Christian who walks with an understanding of their rights and privileges frightens the enemy.

There is no future in your past. Don't dwell on your past look to the future. Have a positive disposition and not a pessimistic one. This takes some effort, but after awhile you'll see the difference. Being positive doesn't mean ignoring bad things that happen to us, we just don't let them keep us down, we let the Lord handle those situations and He will give us the strength and the wisdom to withstand these troubles, and we'll be stronger afterwards.

Be able to receive divine revelation by faith. A lot of times we really sell ourselves short; we either don't think we're worthy to receive revelation, or we just don't think we can. We somehow think that divine revelation just doesn't happen today. Having faith is a key. Faith and logic are opposing forces. We should not be like the world and insist on being logical all the time. The Spirit realm ultimately controls the natural realm, not the other way around.

Determine your priorities. Are your priorities in the proper order? Don't drift through life just trying to make it through each day. Are you focused on material things or things of the Spirit? Material things are okay and God wants us to enjoy them but He wants us to put Him first. Material things have never given me peace and filled that void that only God can fill; but when I put Him first, I enjoy everything, particularly His creation. Not many things are better than camping or enjoying a backyard cookout, or soaking in the scenery on the way to a place we've never been before.

Establish your convictions. You'll struggle until you set your standard for living. You can't fit in with the multitudes anymore; you're going to have to stand out, but you're going to live a quality of life that you never dreamed of. That's because God intended for us to desire high standards. It's hard to explain unless you've tried it.

Me, myself and I, that's who my life used to be centered on, if that's you, get broken to your self-centeredness. You'll be less prone to negative thinking about yourself if...you're not thinking about yourself so much. Once again, that's also because that's part of God's plan to think about others, in fact...to love others as ourselves. One of the biggest single problems in Christian experience, if not the biggest is an unwillingness to die to self interests and self concerns. I have problems with this but I'm gradually shedding some self interests. I've pretty much gotten rid of self concern, maybe not perfectly, but I know that I've got to keep dying to more fully live.

Alright so you're going through a difficult time, presumably depression. I know it's terrible, I know you wonder, "Why me?" This desert that you're wandering through could be and can be God's "decontamination zone" for you. A time to get rid of all of the things that you've been contaminated with, habitual sin, materialism, selfishness, fear, doubt, spiritual laziness, arrogance, neuroses, lack of focus, wrong priorities and the list can be as different and as long as there are insects in your backyard. What an analogy! [3]

Possibly you may not know God, and Jesus Christ as your Savior. All of these things and more were things that were embedded or wrong in my life. But it doesn't have to be depression; or at least depression from chemical imbalance. Many problems and difficulties in our life are not our fault. They're just stuff that happens, and again, "Why me". The book of James gives some nice advice on this subject.

"Dear brothers, is your life full of difficulties and temptations? Then be happy, for when the way is rough, your patience has a chance to grow. So let it grow, and don't try to squirm out of your problems. For when your patience is finally in bloom, then you will be ready for anything, strong in character, full and complete."

"If you want to know what God wants you to do, ask Him and He will surely tell you, for He is always ready to give a bountiful supply of wisdom to all who ask Him; He will not resent it. But when you ask Him be sure that you really expect Him to tell you, for a doubtful mind will be as unsettled as a wave of the sea that is driven and tossed by the wind; and every decision you make will be uncertain, as you turn first this way and then that. If you don't ask with any faith, don't expect the Lord to give you any clear answer."[4]

James 1:2-8

The cross represents two inescapable things: brokenness and humility. Christ did it for us to take away our sins, and I think to show us a way to peace and joy in our life that may not be apparent to us. The human creature has to be born again into a new creation that is broken and humble and willing to be molded and shaped by The Creator. "But whatever is good and perfect comes to us from God, the Creator of all light, and He shines forever without change or shadow. And it was a happy day for Him when He gave us our new lives, through the truth of His Word, and we became, as it were, the first children of His new family."[5]

James 1:17, 18

"Snake bites" (spiritually) come from people's words or writings; for example: reasonings, doubt, flattery and criticism. Snake bites poison your hope your faith, your future, your purpose.[6] I was poisoned by reasonings and doubt for so many years. Faith was not in my vocabulary. Now I see that God wants us to live by Faith.

"The man who finds life will find it through trusting God"[7]

Romans 1:17

Two scriptures that I think are good antidotes for "snake bite" and are a summation of the gospels: 1 John 5:11 and 1 John 5:13

"And what is this that God has said? That He has given us eternal life and that this life is in His Son."[8]

1 John 5:11

"I have written this to you who believe in the Son of God so that you may know that you have eternal life."[9]

1 John 5:13

"And we will never stop thanking God for this: that when we preached to you, you didn't think of the words we spoke as being just our own, but you accepted what we said as the very Word of God – which, of course, it was –and it changed your lives when you believed it."[10]

1 Thessalonians 2:13

Psalm 90, verse 1: "Teach us to number our days and recognize how few they are; help us to spend them as we should."[11]

Psalm 91 has some extraordinary words from God that should help you to really live. Verse 4: "He will shield you with His wings! They will shelter you. His faithful promises are your armor." Verse 14: "For the Lord says, 'Because he loves me, I will rescue him; I will make him great because he trusts in my name.'" And Verse 16: "I will satisfy him with a full life and give him my salvation."[12]

Psalm 92, verse 14: "Even in old age they will still produce fruit and be vital and green."[13]

CHAPTER 29

NO HASSLES

Of course it's impossible to have no hassles, but it is possible to eliminate some and reduce many. Hassles affect our quality of life, and we're different in our ability to handle them adequately. I found that I was a person who needed to really reduce my hassles, and Barbara has the same makeup as I do, so it worked out well for us to make the cuts necessary.

I got rid of my boat. Too much maintenance and too many repairs made it a major hassle for me. I didn't use it that much; maybe six times the first year, three or four times the second year and once or twice the last year. Fishing was out and baseball, soccer and cub scouts were in, and of course an abundance of church activities. I also cut back on collecting old bottles which was very time consuming, especially when places to dig were plentiful. Our activities were family oriented and centered on the home. I found that I was happier when I was doing things that were family oriented and particularly husband – wife oriented. The Bible spends a great deal of time on this subject, so it is a very important subject for Him. We have to have time for each other. Don't let hassles interfere with quality time for your wife. We did not let "hassles" interfere with time spent with our kids. When you say no to someone else, you're saying yes to you wife and kids.[1] In spite of my depression, I was determined not to let these years with my young boys slip away. They needed me and I needed them; and our decision to have Barbara stay home with our kids until they were out of high school was one of the best decisions that we ever made. There's just no substitute for a Christian mother being the primary influence over her child especially in the formative years. They didn't cause us many hassles that's for sure.

We weren't married to our jobs, and we definitely weren't concerned about getting rich. That goes back to getting your priorities in order. Barbara quit desiring a new house, and that was a pretty big hurdle for her to overcome; but we got out of debt faster and hence…less hassles. It's important to remember that many people climbing the ladder of success find that when they get to the top, they find that it was leaning on the wrong wall.[2]

A lot of you aren't going to like to hear this but there came a time when Barbara and I decided that we wanted to tithe. It took a couple of pay raises to be delegated strictly toward that goal, but we did it. Believe it or not it took the heavy load of financial burden away. It changed our life in so many ways, a book could be written on that subject alone. We just always had enough from that time on to cover all of our needs and some of our wants. Things lasted longer, God favored me with a better job, we were able to pay for our kid's college just to name a few, and that's just the financial blessings. The spiritual blessings far out weighed those. We've never regretted that decision to tithe, and I'd highly recommend it.

Some positive things that came from our decision to tithe were:

Set priorities.

Freed up time for prayer and bible-reading.

God preparing us for ministry.

Anonymous gifts.

Thinking of others, not so self-centered.

Allows time for quality parenting.

Charles Spurgeon, when teaching on prayer used to say: "Every promise of Scripture is a writing of God which may be placed before him, 'Do as Thou hast said.' The Creator will not cheat the creature that depends upon His Truth; and far more, the Heavenly Father will not break His own words to His own child." Our forefathers discovered that prayers which plead the clear promises of a covenant-keeping God are guaranteed success. In other words, God always does what He says He will do. It's that simple. We may say, "Do as Thou hast said." Now I am not one to say that we should be demanding that God do anything. I would be inclined to say, "Lord please do as Thou hast said." But the point is God does what He says. If God says in His Word that He will do something, you can count on it, that's part of the nature of God that is different from humans. So when you're going through something and you've got to have something to anchor your soul and your very existence, you can find it in God's Word.

"Forever, O Lord your Word stands firm in heaven. Your faithfulness extends to every generation like the earth you created; it endures by your decree, for everything serves your plans.

I would have despaired and perished unless your love had been my perfect delight. I will never lay aside your laws, for you have used everything to restore my joy and health. I am yours. Save me. For I have tried to live according to your desires. Though the wicked lie along the way to kill me, I will quietly keep my mind upon your promises."[3]

Psalm 119:89-96

I underlined the parts that particularly spoke

to me. I wrote on August 19, 2002, "It is clear to me that God used kidney stones and depression to help me find Him. It is even clearer that God gave me His Word to completely heal me, spiritually. It's also very clear that He sent me Barbara, a pure and Christian woman (and her love for me) to be my forever companion." Just by coincidence, a year to the day later, I was laying in the hospital recovering from kidney cancer surgery. Barbara, had insisted that I go in and see my urologist, whom I hadn't seen in about five or six years. He found three very small malignancies in my left kidney. If I hadn't listened to Barbara, who was lead by the Spirit, I wouldn't be doing so hot right now in 2006. There was no reason for me to go humanly speaking and I was having no symptoms, except for the occasional kidney stone pain. When the cancer was advanced enough to cause me some pain, I would probably have thought that this was just kidney stones. Lesson to be learned: listen to your Godly wife.

About two weeks later we learned a good lesson. We couldn't find the cell phone recharger. The house was searched high and low inside and out two or three times in some places. It was not to be found. I'm talking hours upon hours. God spoke to me and said, "Give it up" or "Give up the search". So I told Barbara, and we quit looking. Almost immediately she asked me to get her the heating pad, so I did. When I picked up the folded heating pad, the recharger fell out at my feet. God said, "You see you struggled for nothing because you would have eventually found it when you went to get the heating pad." So God used a simple little thing to show us a valuable life's lesson. God takes care of things, sometimes we need to quit struggling and surrender to Him.

Anxious thoughts are our natural response to the cares of life. We spend sleepless nights trying to solve complex problems whether it is job-related, or maybe a family matter or a financial need. The Bible says that rather than be weighed down by our concerns, we should turn them over to God and let them rest with him. The way to dismiss our worries and concerns is to dwell on the goodness and care of our Creator, not the difficulties that we have.

"In the multitude of my anxieties within me, your comforts delight my soul."[4]

Psalm 94:19
See also 1 Peter 5:7

We have so many promises and blessings from God that are in His Holy Word, and many people don't realize it. My pastor Kevin Baird told a good story that illustrates this point. In the early part of the 20th century, an ocean liner was entering New York harbor after a trip across the Atlantic. Some crewman found a middle-aged woman fainted and on the floor at the rear of the ship hidden away. When they revived her she told them that her husband had gone to America the year before and he had sent her a ticket to America to join him. From the clothing she wore and her appearance she was obviously not a woman of means. (She was poor). She said her husband sent her no additional money for food and she had brought with her some stale bread and moldy cheese. The Captain noticed a ticket sticking out of her coat pocket. He took it out and looked at it and tears came to his eyes. She had a first-class ticket that entitled her to eat at the Captain's table...all she could eat. She just didn't know what she had.

That's how many Christians are that have never cracked open and studied their Bible. They know they're saved, they know the 10 commandments and that's about it. It's more difficult to realize your blessings when there are just too many hassles in your life.

Chapter 30

Happiness

One of my favorite authors is Selwyn Hughes whom I quote quite a bit. His devotionals have been my favorites for years. One area in which he helped me quite a bit is happiness. He said this, "There is nothing wrong with wanting to be happy it's a natural and valid desire. But the paradoxical truth is that I will never be happy if I am primarily concerned with being happy."

You see, if we make happiness our goal, we're never going to find it, but if we quit running after it, and just be aware that we want it, then it will find its way into our heart. In every situation we have to respond as Christ teaches, to put Him first and respond to that situation as he desires us to. The fact is that as we strive to be what Christ wants us to be, righteous; He rewards us by giving us immeasurable happiness and joy. So Selwyn Hughes' point is: "An obsessive preoccupation with 'happiness' will obscure our understanding of the biblical route to eternal peace and joy." We may think that we attract others to Christ more effectively through our strengths than through our weaknesses. But the Lord used trouble and weakness in Paul's life to teach him to rely on God's power (2 Corinthians 1:9). He testified, "When I am weak, then I am strong" (12:10). When Christians act as if they hardly know what weakness is, needy people often think, "I could never be like that." But when Christians admit they experience Christ's strength in their weakness, they proclaim this hope: "The strength Christ gives to me He can give to you!" Whose strength will you proclaim today – your own, or God's?

Selwyn Hughes

This all applies to me. There's no way that I could have made it these last thirty-two years without God's strength. I had to try, and I had to make choices, and I had to rely on God's promises. But my ability to make it was strictly on God's strength and constantly reminding myself of that fact. Yes I had to rely on God's physical healing through medication, yes I had to admit that I was weak and a sinner, yes I knew that I was in for a long ferocious fight; but you know what? Deep, deep down in my soul I knew that I was worth something. God had created me, and He had left me all of His wonderful promises, and that a secret to life is to grab hold of these promises and overcome with them.

My whole purpose of writing this book is sharing how a weak person, seemingly without hope can become a new creation in Christ. My weakness was one of my greatest blessings, because as Paul said, "When I am weak I am strong."

God's ultimate intention is that we learn through periods of darkness, trusting His Word.

There were many periods of darkness for me, periods of depression when the enemy had me doubting my own salvation. I'm reminded of a scripture:

"Those by the way side are they that hear; then cometh the devil, and taketh away the word out of their hearts, lest they should believe and be saved."[1]

Luke 8:12

And Jesus said to the woman, "Your faith has saved you; go in peace."[2]

Luke 8:50

This is pretty strong proof for salvation by believing the salvation message and not by any human plan.

CHAPTER 31

LIFE TODAY

So here I am thirty two years later and I guess you kind of wonder how I'm doing. Every few months a little depression and doubt tries to creep back in on me, but it's quickly debunked, after a little reflection on the Word and all that I've learned the hard way. The sky is blue again; the trees and the grass are green again. In the deepest of my depression, the whole world seemed to be colored dark and grey. When I was depressed, I didn't want to be around people, especially happy people. Now I like being with people, the more simple-minded the better. I don't mean that as a negative thing, but quite the opposite. Where I could take or leave children, even before I was depressed, now I love kids and spent over twenty years ministering to children in Kid's Church.

Life is wonderful, the way God means for it to be. My life is based completely on faith in God and Jesus Christ and their Word. What I am looking forward to during this life are the riches of eternal life. Being with Jesus forever is my reason for being now. All of my personality trusts in the Goodness of

God, and any difficulties of life only serve to stretch my faith and make it grow.

I don't worry all of the time like I used to, I don't have any feelings of insecurity or inadequacy like I used to. The fear of death was conquered long ago, so I don't fear any thing at all. Money is something to be used for good and not to be hoarded or squandered. The more it's used for good, the more I have. We always have enough. I don't have as many kidney stones, not anywhere near as I used to have, and it's been two years since my kidney cancer surgery with no signs of a recurrence. I go to the gym three times a week and spend thirty minutes on the elliptical trainer and twenty to thirty minutes on the various weight training machines. I've added fifteen pounds of muscle and feel great. Barbara and I have been married now for almost thirty four years and we're more in love than ever. She is my best friend (next to Jesus). I make her laugh as often as possible, and she's the greatest with finances and keeping the house running.

Looking back now it doesn't seem like I've been through a nightmare or lived a traumatic life, but more like I've had a really good learning experience that has changed my life and made it more fruitful than I could have ever imagined. It's true that adversity comes so that we can grow. Anytime I am tempted to go over in my mind all that was required to deliver me from that old existence, the Holy Spirit tells me that there is no need to go back over God's plan, methods and instruction that delivered me from that bondage; but every time I do I discover that faith in God's Word brings me the Blessed Assurance of Eternal Life.

I wrote on October 16, 2004, "I have found that whenever God speaks to us through His Word or in our inner man, we are not to reason, debate or ask ourselves if what He has said is logical. When God speaks we are not to rationalize. Our minds and emotions are poor substitutions for God's Word and leading when it comes to getting directions.

"...but you accepted what we said as the very word of God – which of course it was – and it changed your life when you believed it."[1]

1 Thessalonians 2:13

I wrote on December 14, 2004, "God will strengthen me to meet whatever challenge lies ahead. When you're going through something difficult, the hardest thing for me is the uncertainty – how it's going to turn out. That's where we have to leave it in the hands of God. One thing is certain; He will carry us through all the way to our Heavenly home with Him."

It's not God's responsibility to keep me happy every waking hour, without me doing anything.[2] I've learned to be joyful in every circumstance. If there's nothing much in particular going on I rejoice – I get a breather, I can even take a nap. When I work, I work hard but I don't have to be productive every waking hour. When I'm not working, I don't have to be entertained. I happen to enjoy being with my wife and enjoying nature in my backyard and sunsets and just being alive. That's one of the good things that came out of fighting depression for so many years, a great appreciation for the simple life.

I am convinced that God's will for me is good and will happen for me in the future, and I am determined that circumstances will not change the outlook on my life. God is using me in whatever way he chooses; I don't get into comparing myself with other people and how God is using them. We're all doing our unique "something" for God. So my life is inherently useful and that is immensely satisfying. There's no wondering about the meaning of life for me. Presently God wants me to help hurting people by sharing my struggles with depression. I sincerely hope and pray that it helps someone, that it gets them on the road to wholeness sooner than if they had not read this.

I relentlessly believe God. Nothing can deter me from this; it's a part of me. It's more natural than breathing. The evidence is unequivocal.

Eternal life is for the asking and receiving. You don't have to fear death and the unknown. We are all eternal beings and we're going to be somewhere forever. We're on earth for an average of three score and ten, but what is that to eternity somewhere else. You might as well make it Eternal life in heaven.

Jesus said, "Any man who comes to me, I will in no wise cast out."[3] Simply put is it not? You can be adopted into the family of God simply by coming to His Son. Everyone will have an opportunity to make the choice to accept salvation or choose to refuse it. It's a free gift although it didn't come without a price. Jesus said, "I come into the world not to condemn it but to save it."[4] He came to earth, He told us what we needed to know and then He willingly died on the cross to pay the price for our salvation just as He said He would. I have forgiveness for every evil thing that I've ever thought done or said. It's God's gift to you and I.

Chapter 32

What if I'm not a Christian ?

If you're not a Christian and you bought this book because you were depressed and curious, you might be thinking, "Well all of this sounds good, but it's all predicated on the fact that God exists." Well that's true and I'll devote a little space in this book to discuss this, although some very well-written works have been written on this subject, including *The Case for Christ* and *The Case for Creator*.

First of all, you know in your heart that you are no cosmic accident. If you go back far enough, something had to come from nothing. If you're a believer in the Big Bang theory, where did all of the gas for the explosion come from?

The earth is the perfect distance from the sun. If it were any closer, we'd burn up and any farther away and we'd freeze. He put the earth at just the right angle to cause seasons. If we didn't revolve around the sun, just as we do, we would have ice ages that would make animal life impossible. The planet Jupiter shields us from comets and the moon give us light at night and cause tides that are just right.

You can't forget that gravity is just right for our bodies. We don't float off the earth and we don't feel so heavy that we can hardly move.

How about the miraculous design of our own human bodies? How about the brain controlling our involuntary functions and the reproductive process? What about thoughts and emotions – accidents? What about that which is in us that gives us knowledge of good and evil?

The process by which we can see should astound the most severe critic. Nerves that can carry images that are around us to our brain so that we can see, is slightly more than I can conceive of as happening quite by accident.

The variety of animals, birds, fish and insects that are in this world seems to have taken a bit of imagination. The existence of tens of thousands of different species with no Designer is beyond belief in my opinion. It takes more faith to believe that all of creation is an accident with no designer than it does to believe that there is a Designer.

One couple who started out as atheists, became Christians after a long period of resisting all that they had learned. The wife eventually told her husband, "I settled the matter several days ago but I was afraid to tell you. All the things we studied and learned finally convinced me about the Bible, about Christ, and about my need --- our need ---for Him. A few days ago I knew that I was completely convinced." She had already prayed to receive God's gift of forgiveness and eternal life. "And that started the biggest adventure of our lives." They became missionaries for thirty-three years in Bangladesh.

Oxford's Alister McGrath pointed out that all world views require faith. "The truth claims of atheism simply cannot be proved, he said. "How do we know there is no God? The simple fact of the matter is that atheism is a faith, which draws conclusions that go beyond the available evidence."

On the other hand, the available evidence from the latest scientific research is convincing more and more scientists that facts support faith as never before. "The age-old notion that there is more to existence than meets the eye suddenly looks like fresh thinking again," said journalist Gregg Easterbrook. "We are entering the greatest era of science-religion fusion since the Enlightenment last attempted to reconcile the two."

To many people, including physicist Paul Davies, this is a shocking and unexpected development. "It may seem bizarre," he said, "but in my opinion science offers a surer path to God than religion."

Added nanoscientist James Tour of Rice University: "Only a rookie who knows nothing about science would say science takes away from faith. If you really study science, it will bring you closer to God." Astrophysicist and priest George Coyne put it this way: "Nothing we learn about the universe threatens our faith. It only enriches it."

For Polkinghorne, who achieved acclaim as a mathematical physicist at Cambridge before becoming a full-time minister, the same kind of thinking he uses in science has helped him draw life-changing conclusions about God:

No one has ever seen a quark, and we believe that no one ever will. They are so tightly bound to each other inside the protons and neutrons that nothing can make them break out on their own. Why, then, do I believe in these invisible quarks?...In summary, it's because quarks make sense of a lot of direct physical evidence…I wish to engage in a similar strategy with regard to the unseen reality of God. His existence makes sense of many aspects of our knowledge and experience: the order and fruitfulness of the physical world; the multilayered character of reality; the almost universal human experiences of worship and hope; the phenomenon of Jesus Christ (including his resurrection). I think that very similar thought processes are involved in both cases. I do not believe that I shift in some strange intellectual way when I move from science to religion…In their search for truth, science and faith are intellectual cousins under the skin."[1]

Was Jesus a real person? Jewish historians wrote about Him as well as the Roman historian Josephus, from the first century, so there is an independent record of the existence of Jesus other than the Bible.

Hundreds of years before Jesus was born; prophets foretold the coming of the Messiah, or the Anointed One, who would redeem God's people. In effect, the Old Testament prophecies created a fingerprint that only the true Messiah could fit. That gave Israel a way to rule out impostors and validate the credentials of the true Messiah. Against astronomical odds ---by one estimate, one chance in a trillion, trillion, trillion, trillion, trillion, trillion, trillion, trillion, trillion, trillion, trillion, trillion, trillion --- Jesus and only Jesus throughout history, matched the prophetic fingerprint. This confirms Jesus' identity to an incredible degree of certainty.[2]

The Dead Sea Scrolls were written centuries before Christ was born and contain portions of the Old Testament that prophesied about the birth, life and death of Christ. All of the hundreds of prophecies about Christ came true so we can ascertain that all of the other prophesies that are yet fulfilled will come true as well. Let's take just ten of these prophecies and assign a probability to each one that it could happen randomly to one person by chance.

That He would be born in Bethlehem, a small Judean village. There are hundreds of small Judean villages, but we'll assign a probability of 1 in 100 that a particular man would be born in Bethlehem.

That He would be called a Nazarene. Again there are hundreds of towns, villages and cities in Israel, but we'll assign a probability of 1 in 100 that a particular man would live in Nazareth.

That He would ride on a donkey's colt. Riding a donkey would certainly not be unusual, but a donkey's colt would be. We will assign a modest probability of 1 in 10 for this to happen by chance to a particular man.

That He would be buried in a rich man's grave. To be buried in someone else's grave is unusual and a rich man's at that, but we'll assign a probability of 1 in 20 for this to happen by chance to a particular man.

That He would have lots cast for His clothes. This is certainly an unusual occurrence and we could easily assign a probability of 1 in a 1,000 but we'll assign a modest value of 1 in 100.

That He was spat upon. An unusual occurrence, although not rare, I think to happen by chance to a particular man warrants a probability of 1 in 10.

Not one of his bones shall be broken. This rates a higher probability. I will give it a 1 in 2 chance that this could happen by chance to one particular man.

They pierced his hands and feet. This was prophesied hundreds of years before the Romans came into power and introduced crucifixion as a means of execution. I will give this a probability of 1 in 100 that this could happen to one particular man by chance.

He was given gall. I will give this a modest value of 1 in 10 even though this is a horrible tasting concoction which is used to dull the senses somewhat. Jesus refused it however.

He was counted among thieves. This rates a much lower probability to happen by chance because the Messiah was understood to be a King, and for a King to be counted among thieves would have to be considered highly unusual. Although I could arguably justify a much lower probability, I will assign one of 1 in 100.

To calculate the probability of all of these predictions coming true for one particular man by chance we have to multiply the probabilities:

100 x 100 x 10 x 20 x 100 x 10 x 2 x 100 x 10 x 100 = 400,000,000,000,000.

That's one chance in four hundred trillion! That's only 10 prophecies out of many. The men that had this power to predict events happening centuries into the future had to have God's help.

To illustrate possibility of these ten events happening to one man by chance, consider this. A golden wedding ring is dropped from an airplane at 35,000 feet into an ocean. The plane returns to land takes on the blindfolded owner of the ring. The owner of the ring has a rod and reel with a weighted hook and enough line to reach the bottom of the deepest ocean. Whenever the person desires, the hook is lowered. The chances of the ring being snagged are about the same as the probability we calculated about Christ.

"We have better historical documentation for Jesus than for the founder of any other ancient religion," said Edwin Yamauchi of Miami University, a leading expert on ancient history. Sources from outside the Bible corroborate that many people believed Jesus performed healings and was the Messiah, and He was crucified, and that despite this shameful death, His followers, who believed He was still alive, worshipped Him as God.

One expert documented thirty-nine ancient sources that corroborate more than one hundred facts concerning Jesus' life, teachings, crucifixion and resurrection. Seven secular sources and several early Christian creeds concern the deity of Jesus a doctrine "definitely present in the earliest church," according to Gary Habermas, the scholar who wrote *The Historical Jesus*.[3]

Perhaps you're a non-Christian and you need something miraculous, that you can see, with your own eyes, to get your interest. You need something that you could actually touch, if you were allowed to. If you could see this miraculous object, you would be interested enough to accept Jesus Christ as your Lord and Savior and see what God's Word says. Although there is not a lot of press given to it, there is such an object that has baffled scientists from around the world for decades, it has mystified people for centuries and it can be traced back through history to the time of Christ. It is believed to be the burial cloth of Jesus Christ. It is called the Shroud of Turin, because that is where it resided for hundreds of years. It is a fourteen foot long piece of cloth with the front and back images of a crucified man. The image is a photographic negative and when a picture is taken of it the negative reveals an astounding three-dimensional image. The image is not painted and scientists have concluded that the image is only on the outermost fibers of the cloth. Scientists say that the image appears to have been made by something similar to a scorch or some sort of burst of energy. The image bears all of the marks of the unusual crucifixion of Christ, the bleeding from a crown of thorns, a spear wound in the side in addition to the nails piercings in the hands and feet. In addition there are over one hundred scourge marks from a beating with a type of whip that the Romans used in the first century.

The image isn't painted but if it were it would be the greatest work of art in the history of the world. Leonardo da Vinci or Michelangelo couldn't have painted it. The edges of the image fade into nothing and there is nothing on the cloth but discolored fibers.

There have been many well written books on the Shroud of Turin and if reading them gets you wondering if there is something to Christianity or that maybe there really is a God; then it was well worth my mentioning it in this book. One excellent book on the subject is *The Blood and the Shroud*.[4]

Lee Strobel has written many excellent books including, *The Case for a Creator*, *The Case for Faith* and *The Case for Christ*. In *The Case for Christ*, he describes historical evidence for the miracles of Jesus, especially his resurrection from the dead.

Romans 1:20 tells us that God's eternal power and divine nature can be seen and understood through things that are made, and this is the reason that humanity is without excuse.

The New York Times recently published a famous quote by physicist Freeman Dyson, who looked at the evidence that the world has been fine-tuned and said, "The universe in some sense must have known that we were coming."

Paul Davies said in his book, *Superforce: The Search for a Grand Unified Theory of Nature*, "In the case of a crossword puzzle, it would never occur to us to suppose that the words just happen to fall into a consistent interlocking pattern by accident."

If you're not a Christian and you're questioning what life is all about and why do you have to be depressed, take a few quiet moments and soak in these words so beautifully expressed by Alister McGrath, and let them set your sails on a new course toward wholeness and claim all of the wonderful promises God has for us in His written Word:

"Many have found that the awesome sight of the star-studded heavens evoke a sense of wonder, an awareness of transcendence, that is charged with spiritual significance. Yet the distant shimmering of stars does not itself create this sense of longing; it merely exposes what is already there, They are catalysts for our spiritual insights, revealing our emptiness and compelling us to ask whether and how this void might be filled.

Might our true origins and destiny somehow lie beyond those stars? Might there be a homeland from which we are presently exiled and to which we secretly long to return? Might not our accumulation of discontent and disillusionment with our present existence be a pointer to another land where our true destiny lies and which is able to make its presence felt now in this haunting way?

Suppose that this is not where we are meant to be but that a better land is at hand? We don't belong here. We have somehow lost our way. Would not this make our existence both strange and splendid? Strange because it is not where our true destiny lies; splendid because it points ahead to where that real hope might be found. The beauties of the night skies or a glorious sunset are important pointers to the origins and the ultimate fulfillment of our heart's deepest desires. But if we mistake the signpost for what is signposted, we will attach our hopes and longings to lesser goals, which cannot finally quench our thirst for meaning."[5]

CHAPTER 33

WHAT I HAVE LEARNED

We read in Hebrews:

"The fundamental fact of existence is that this trust in God, this faith, is the firm foundation under everything that makes life worth living. It's our handle on what we can't see."[1]

The greatest power of faith lies not in how we think we might use it to conquer challenges that we're sure a loving God would not put in our path, but in how we live with courage and purpose in the midst of devastating problems with no foreseeable solution and serious questions with no foreseeable answer.

There have been times that I felt like Job in Job 6:10:

"But it is still my consolation that I rejoice in unsparing pain, that I have not denied the words of the Holy One."[2]

Ralph Waldo Emerson wrote over 150 years ago, "And by slowly listening we shall hear the right word...Place yourself in the middle of the stream of power and wisdom which flows into your life. Then without effort you are impelled to truth and to perfect contentment…A believing love will relieve us of a vast load of care. Oh, my brothers, God exists!"

Before my depression, I now understand that I led a very shallow life. I was also very insecure and fearful. My general outlook was that everything that went wrong in my life was because of something that I did. Everything was my fault, a result of my shortcomings. I felt very inferior to everyone else. Where did all of these feelings come from? I don't know for sure, but I believe most of it was a chemical imbalance, some of it was my own personality and some was learned during my early development. But you know it really doesn't matter. We come as a package deal; we are what we are imperfections and all, life experiences included. All of us have our own set of circumstances that we have to deal with, and many of us don't know that we don't have to manage this alone. There is a Heavenly Father that is waiting for our call for help. These imperfect lives that we have are not meant for our demise, but for our eternal benefit. Their purpose is to make us realize that we need something else, something that is not available from earthly sources. Actually, even the medical procedures and medications that we have available are from God. But to be truly whole, we need God and His Son, Jesus Christ. The words of Jesus have taken away all of my fears, worries, doubts and anxieties. There is no other way that this was possible.

As I said earlier, in 2003 I was diagnosed with kidney cancer. There were three lesions on the outside of my left kidney which were discovered with a CT scan. Other tests were made to determine if cancer was in my bones or lungs. Fortunately it wasn't. The surgery was performed and the tumors were removed, and two years later, I have had four or five scans which have all been negative. Years ago, I would have freaked out, thought it was because of something that I did and that I was being punished for. In 2004 I had a TURP performed due to an enlarged prostate. My urologist took me off of my long-time anti-depressant, amitriptyline (Elavil) and put me on Paroxetine (Paxil). That was a little scary. (Would it work as well?) It did, in fact, with much less side effects. There was no fear; I just trusted that God would get me through. Barbara told me that she was a little concerned about switching medications.

I have been through the worst, and I got through it, so I live completely free of fear. I treasure life because I see how fragile it is and how it really is out of any control we think we have. I used to rely on myself alone, and that made me weak; now I rely on Jesus alone and that makes me strong.

One fear that I used to have, and one that most people that have been through depression have is that they may fall into a depression again. Our carnal mind is not God's Word so anytime I feel a fear cropping up, I think of one of my favorite scriptures and the fear is immediately gone. There really is supernatural healing through God's Word and it is completely natural to trust God and believe in His Word even though we don't understand how it all works and fits together.

I don't let criticisms control me. If I'm doing God's will and believing His Son and being led by His Spirit, why should I be concerned about what men say or think? I care in the sense that I don't want to make anyone stumble. Comparing myself to others that I admire and respect is something I don't do anymore. I am a unique child of God and He loves me unconditionally. When I stumble, He's there to pick me up and get me going again. When I stumble I don't let it get me down for long periods, but I ask God's forgiveness and I get over it. I dwell on God's future for me and by doing that I have become free of issues in my past.

I can do what Jesus says I can do. Read the gospels again or for the first time as the case may be, and you will be amazed. Jesus said that if you didn't take His Word for it, then at least believe what He said, and that He was sent by God because of the miracles that He did. No one could have done those miracles if He hadn't been sent by God.

I now see that there are two types of persons, those who live by what is thrown at them and those that live by faith and create their future. Everything starts with a choice.

In my case for example, I became depressed to the point that I didn't think I could go on another day, and yet each day I did. At that point it was simply a choice to keep going on in spite of the pain, in hopes that I would get okay; even though I had no idea of what was wrong with me or if I could get back to where I was. Now in hindsight, I realize that "where I was" wasn't so hot. But my point is that I chose to endure the pain until I could find my way out of the condition that I was in. There was no spiritual insight to my thought process or decision making.

These days my choices are all faith-based. I know that all sickness and disease are a result of the fall of Adam. The enemy, Satan has limited powers to make us miserable through all kinds of tactics, not the least of which are disease, lies, deceits, fears, confusion, doubt, depression and anxiety. I know that God wins the battle by turning Satan's attacks to achieve our ultimate good by causing us to seek Him.

God isn't really concerned about our happiness. Now that may sound a little harsh, but let me explain. He wants us to be happy, but eternally happy. If we somehow escaped all discomfort down here in our short duration on earth, we may not seek God and thereby miss out on eternal happiness. A lot of people don't see it that way; they are convinced that God should not allow any suffering in the world and just make sure everyone gets to heaven. Since He doesn't, it causes them to question God's existence. God, however, wants his ultimate creation to love Him voluntarily; He doesn't want a bunch of robotic creatures that love Him and choose Him because that is the way that they are programmed.

There is as I said all kinds of suffering in the world. I do not minimize any type of suffering; it all hurts terribly when you are the one going through it. But where the enemy really attacks us the most effectively for his purpose is in our minds. That is why depression is so vicious. It can cause us to lose hope and to immobilize us, preventing us from discovering the truth. But it can have the opposite affect and cause us to seek the Truth. The mind is the battlefield. Joyce Meyer's book, *Battlefield of the Mind*, is an excellent book on this topic and I highly recommend it.

A huge truth that I've learned is that if I seek

happiness in the things of this world, I'll never find it; but if I seek it in the future with God I will.

I've learned to be exceedingly grateful that there is help for me. I've learned that I can live a normal and happy life just as long as I stay healthy and use all of the therapies God has made available. I'm completely powerless, on my own, over depression and the problems that arose from depression had nothing to do with my character, my circumstances, my attitude, or my faith.

Keep a journal if you don't already have one. A journal can be a notebook of any kind in which you record your thoughts, insights, hopes, fears, prayers and so forth over a period of time. One value of a journal is that it can provide, retrospectively, a vivid reminder of how you were doing during certain periods of your life.[3]

I know that God loves me and wanted me to win my battle with depression just as He wants you to win your battle over depression. I pray that when people see you and I and how we have progressed they will want to know the reason for the victory that we have in our life.

Hurricane Katrina just ravaged the Gulf Coast and in the images shown day after day and night after night show the splintered homes and oak trees sprinkled throughout standing tall. I thought how

God's creation weathered the storm, but man's failed miserably. It's the same with life. Build your life on God's Word because it lasts.

I've learned not to make life so complicated. God didn't intend for it to be. It's better to lead a simple life. The Greek definition of simplicity is: "singleness of vision, clear, focus, not complex." We should not complex our lives up. We complex everything. Some people complex themselves right out of the will of God. God uses simple-minded people to get His work done. The twelve disciples were simple guys. They hung on everything that Jesus said. When Jesus asked the twelve if they were going to leave him like some other followers, Peter answered, "Master, to whom shall we go? You alone have the words that give eternal life."[4] Obey God. Believe God. That's simple and it's my "formula", if you will, for life. God will do what His Word says.

It would be great if I hadn't needed medication to help me, but thanks to the pills, I am able to hear what God wants to say to me. I can function physically. I see that my depression has allowed me to take part in God's plan, which for me is to help others who suffer from depression. I don't see how it could possibly be a "failing" in God's eyes for me to overcome my circumstances and help others to do the same.

CHAPTER 34

MEMORIES

It's been a long journey and as I look back on it and remember all of the events leading up to now I see very clearly where I was and where I am and the pain and joys of getting here. I think to myself, "Was it worth it?" The answer is a resounding -Yes! I've also wondered, "Was there a purpose to it, did it result in anything good?" Again the answer is a huge - Yes. The mental, physical and emotional pain was all worth it because I am stronger, I am wiser and I am more sensitive to the needs of others. I humbled myself, reached out for help wherever I could find it, and the process I found the One whom many blame for their troubles. My transformation was nothing short of a miraculous transformation by God through the redemptive power of His Son's crucifixion, and this transformation happens in the lives of others every day. I started seeing that my greatest strength was my great weakness, because it made me need God. He is my only strength. He is the Source of the healing in the anti-depressants and He is the Source of the healing in His Eternal Word.

The enemy tries to take everything away from us that we think is important, through the pit of depression. I know that the fear and depression that enveloped me made me feel more dead than alive. God allowed me to go through it so that I could find out what is truly important. My most precious possessions now are His promises. I don't take anything for granted now; I am definitely a new creation now with a whole different perspective on life and a completely different set of values. What was once important then is not so important now and vice versa.

My experiences and memories also have made me uniquely "qualified" to help others struggling with their own set of circumstances and depression. That's why I'm writing about my life-long journey with depression, to let others that follow know that they too can emerge from the pit they're in and manage to have quite a rewarding life that is, in reality, a life that is worth living. The life I'm talking about far surpasses anything that anyone could imagine, without the help of the Holy Spirit. From courage to joy to purpose, all wrapped in love, is a road paved by Him.

God can use a sensitive Christian to be a rich blessing in the life of one who knows pain and sorrow…Someone has said, "To have suffered much is like knowing many languages. It gives the sufferer access to many more people."

Billy Graham
Unto the Hills

Events in life result in memories. These memories can be wonderful and happy or they can result in strongholds of negative emotions and embedded lies.

"He has sent me to proclaim freedom for the prisoners and recovery of sight for the blind, to release the oppressed."[1]

Luke 4:18

Anyone that feels called to help suffering believers or unbelievers is in very good company. I don't know why God has given me this calling to help the oppressed, but it's very satisfying to know that I'm doing one of the things God put me on this earth to do.

At times I wonder, *Who do I think I am thinking that I should share my story, I'm not anybody special?* But I do think that God walked with me on this journey, and I believe that He wanted me to share my story. I'm being obedient. I'm not the same person, not even close, yet I have weaknesses and still need Christ for every second of existence. I still struggle with negative thoughts trying to creep in, but I don't panic, freak out and go into a tailspin for days, weeks, months or years. I understand what is the source of the negative thoughts and I overcome them with the Word of God. That's my simple message, and I will overcome daily with that simple plan that God has made for us until He calls me home.

NOTES

Chapter 1. My Struggle

1. The Holy Bible, People's Parallel Edition, Living translation.
2. David B. Biebel, D. Min. & Harold G. Koenig, M.D., "New Light on Depression".

Chapter 2. Anxiety

1. www.healthyplace.com.
2. www.support4hope.com.
3. The Holy Bible, People's Parallel Edition, Living translation.
4. Ibid.
5. Ibid.
6. Ibid.
7. Ibid.
8. David B. Biebel, D. Min. & Harold G. Koenig, M.D., "New Light on Depression", 36.

Chapter 3. What Causes Depression?

1. David B. Biebel, D. Min. & Harold G. Koenig, M.D., "New Light on Depression", 39.
2. Ibid, 37 – 38.
3. Ibid, 38.
4. www.walking-wounded.net.

5. The Holy Bible, People's Parallel Edition, Living translation.
6. www.healthyplace.com.

Chapter 4. How Does Depression Make You Feel?

1. David B. Biebel, D. Min. & Harold G. Koenig, M.D., "New Light on Depression".
2. www.support4hope.com.

Chapter 5. Treatment

1. David B. Biebel, D. Min. & Harold G. Koenig, M.D., "New Light on Depression".
2. Ibid.,

Chapter 6. God's Word

1. The Holy Bible, People's Parallel Edition, Living translation.
2. Ibid.
3. Ibid.
4. Ibid.
5. Ibid.
6. Ibid.
7. Ibid.
8. Ibid.
9. Ibid.
10. Ibid.
11. Ibid.

12. Ibid.
13. Ibid.
14. Ibid.
15. Ibid.
16. Ibid.
17. Ibid.
18. Ibid.
19. Ibid.
20. David B. Biebel, D. Min. & Harold G. Koenig, M.D., "New Light on Depression".

Chapter 7. Obsessive Thoughts

1. The Holy Bible, People's Parallel Edition, Living translation.
2. Ibid.
3. Ibid.
4. Ibid.
5. Ibid.
6. Ibid.
7. Ibid.
8. Ibid.
9. Ibid.

Chapter 8. A Defining Moment

1. David B. Biebel, D. Min. & Harold G. Koenig, M.D., "New Light on Depression",
2. The Holy Bible, People's Parallel Edition, Living translation.

3. Ibid.

Chapter 9. Forgive Yourself

1. The Holy Bible, People's Parallel Edition, Living translation.
2. Ibid.
3. Ibid.
4. Ibid.
5. Ibid.
6. Ibid.
7. Ibid.
8. Ibid.
9. Ibid.
10. Ibid.
11. Ibid.

Chapter 10. Who Suffers With Depression?

1. Clark E. Barshinger, Lojan E. LaRowe, and Andres Tapia, "The Gospel According to Prozac," Christianity Today (14 August, 1995), 35.
2. Siang-Yang Tan, "The ABCs of Depression: A Review of the Basics," Christian Counseling Today (Fall 1995), 10.
3. The Random House Unabridged Dictionary, 1967.
4. "Fighting the Stigma," Newsweek (20 May 1996), 22-23.

5. F. Duane Lindsey, The Servant Songs (Chicago: Moody, 1985), 116.
6. The New Dictionary of Thoughts, 1936 ed., s.v. "Melancholy."
7. Vera Phillips and Edwin Roberstson, J.B. Phillips: The Wounded Healer Grand Rapids, MI: Eerdmans, 1984), 110.
8. John White, The Masks of Melancholy (Downers Grove, IL: InterVarsity, 1982), 77-82.
9. Ibid., 18.
10. The New Dictionary of Thoughts, s.v. "Despair."
11. White, 25.
12. Ibid., 103-125.
13. Leslie Stevenson, Seven Theories of Human Nature (New York: Oxford, 1987), 6.
14. White, 53.
15. Ibid.
16. Ibid., 41.
17. Ibid., 45.
18. Ibid., 47.
19. Ibid., 49.
20. Ibid.
21. Ibid., 220.
22. National Institute of Mental Health, "Depression: What you need to know" (Indianapolis: Eli Lilly, n.d.), 1-3.
23. Ibid., 9.

24. The Holy Bible, People's Parallel Edition, Living translation.

Chapter 11. Growing Pains

1. The Holy Bible, People's Parallel Edition, Living translation.

Chapter 12. My Family

1. The Holy Bible, People's Parallel Edition, Living translation.
2. Ibid.
3. Ibid.

Chapter 13. Don't Lose Hope, Find The Will To Live and See A Doctor.

1. David B. Biebel, D. Min. & Harold G. Koenig, M.D., "New Light on Depression", 68 – 69.

Chapter 14. Turn To God For Help, Standing Firm Against The Enemy, Bitterness and Unforgiveness.

1. The Holy Bible, People's Parallel Edition, Living translation.
2. Ibid.
3. David B. Biebel, D. Min. & Harold G. Koenig, M.D., "New Light on Depression", 276.
4. The Holy Bible, People's Parallel Edition, Living translation.

Chapter 15. Getting Over It, Getting It and Getting Better.

1. The Holy Bible, People's Parallel Edition, Living translation.
2. David B. Biebel, D. Min. & Harold G. Koenig, M.D., "New Light on Depression", 190.
3. Ibid., 191 – 192.
4. The Holy Bible, People's Parallel Edition, Living translation.

Chapter 16. Never Give Up

Chapter 17. God's Healing Dirt

1. www.support4hope.com.
2. Ibid.
3. David B. Biebel, D. Min. & Harold G. Koenig, M.D., "New Light on Depression", 192.
4. Ibid., 265.

Chapter 18. The Emotional War

1. Kevin Baird, M. Div., D. Min.

Chapter 19. The Spiritual War – You Can't Lose

1. Dr. Kevin Baird, M. Div., D. Min.
2. The Holy Bible, People's Parallel Edition, Living translation.
3. Ibid.

4. Ibid.
5. The Holy Bible, People's Parallel Edition, King James translation.

Chapter 20. Nothing Is Impossible

1. Dr. Kevin Baird, M. Div., D. Min.
2. The Holy Bible, People's Parallel Edition.
3. The Holy Bible, People's Parallel Edition, King James translation.

Chapter 21. A Renovation Project

1. The Holy Bible, People's Parallel Edition, Living translation.
2. Ibid.
3. Ibid.
4. Ibid.
5. Ibid.
6. Ibid.
7. Ibid.
8. Ibid.
9. Ibid.
10. Ibid.
11. Ibid.
12. Ibid.
13. Ibid.
14. Dr. Kevin Baird, M. Div., D. Min.

Chapter 22. A New Thing

1. The Holy Bible, People's Parallel Edition, Living translation.
2. Dr. Kevin Baird, M. Div., D. Min.
3. Dr. Kevin Baird, M. Div., D. Min.
4. The Holy Bible, People's Parallel Edition, Living translation.
5. Ibid.
6. Ibid.
7. Ibid.
8. Ibid.
9. Ibid.
10. Ibid.
11. Dr. Kevin Baird, M. Div., D. Min.
12. The Holy Bible, People's Parallel Edition, Living translation.
13. Dr. Kevin Baird, M. Div., D. Min.

Chapter 23. Reasonings and Doubt

1. The Holy Bible, People's Parallel Edition, Living translation.
2. Ibid.
3. Ibid
4. Ibid.
5. Ibid.
6. Ibid.
7. Ibid.
8. Ibid.

9. Ibid.

Chapter 24. Psalm 73

Chapter 25. Your Spouse

1. www.walking-wounded.net.
2. The Holy Bible, People's Parallel Edition, Living translation.

Chapter 26. Your Kids

1. The Holy Bible, People's Parallel Edition, Living translation.

Chapter 27. Obsessive Thoughts 2

1. The Holy Bible, People's Parallel Edition, Living translation.
2. Ibid.

Chapter 28. Really Living

1. Dr. Kevin Baird, M. Div., D. Min.
2. The Holy Bible, People's Parallel Edition, Living translation.
3. Dr. Kevin Baird, PHD in a Sunday service.
4. The Holy Bible, People's Parallel Edition, Living translation.
5. Ibid.
6. Dr. Kevin Baird, M. Div., D. Min.

7. The Holy Bible, People's Parallel Edition, Living translation.
8. Ibid.
9. Ibid.
10. Ibid.
11. Ibid.
12. Ibid.
13. Ibid.

Chapter 29. No Hassles

1. Jan Dravecky, "A Joy I'd Never Known.", 201.
2. Dr. Kevin Baird, M. Div., D. Min.
3. The Holy Bible, People's Parallel Edition, Living translation.
4. Ibid.

Chapter 30. Happiness

1. The Holy Bible, People's Parallel Edition, Living translation.
2. Ibid.

Chapter 31. Life Today

1. The Holy Bible, People's Parallel Edition, Living translation.
2. Dr. Kevin Baird, M. Div., D. Min.
3. The Holy Bible, People's Parallel Edition, Living translation.
4. Ibid.

Chapter 32. What if I'm Not A Christian?

1. John Polkinghorne, Quarks, Chaos and Christianity, 98 -100.
2. Lee Strobel, The Case for a Creator, 296.
3. Ibid., 294.
4. Ian Wilson, The Blood Of The Shroud.
5. Lee Strobel, The Case for a Creator, 292.

Chapter 33. What Have I Learned?

1. The Holy Bible, People's Parallel Edition, Living translation.
2. Ibid.
3. David B. Biebel, D. Min. & Harold G. Koenig, M.D., "New Light on Depression", 192.
4. The Holy Bible, People's Parallel Edition, Living translation.
5. Ibid.

Chapter 34. Memories.

1. The Holy Bible, People's Parallel Edition, Living translation.

BIBLIOGRAPHY

1. The Holy Bible, People's Parallel Edition, Living translation.
2. David B. Biebel, D. Min. & Harold G. Koenig, M.D., "New Light on Depression".
3. www.healthyplace.com.
4. www.support4hope.com.
5. www.walking-wounded.net.
6. Clark E. Barshinger, Lojan E. LaRowe, and Andres Tapia, "The Gospel According to Prozac," Christianity Today (14 August, 1995)
7. Siang-Yang Tan, "The ABCs of Depression: A Review of the Basics," Christian Counseling Today (Fall 1995).
8. The Random House Unabridged Dictionary, 1967.
9. "Fighting the Stigma," Newsweek (20 May 1996)
10. F. Duane Lindsey, The Servant Songs (Chicago: Moody, 1985)
11. The New Dictionary of Thoughts, 1936 ed., s.v. "Melancholy."
12. Vera Phillips and Edwin Roberstson, J.B. Phillips: The Wounded Healer Grand Rapids MI: Eerdmans, 1984)

13. John White, The Masks of Melancholy (Downers Grove, IL: InterVarsity, 1982)
14. The New Dictionary of Thoughts, s.v. "Despair."
15. Leslie Stevenson, Seven Theories of Human Nature (New York: Oxford, 1987).
16. National Institute of Mental Health, "Depression: What you need to know" (Indianapolis: Eli Lilly, n.d.)
17. Dr. Kevin Baird, in a Sunday service.
18. Jan Dravecky, "A Joy I'd Never Known."
19. John Polkinghorne, Quarks, Chaos and Christianity
20. Lee Strobel, The Case for a Creator
21. Ian Wilson, The Blood Of The Shroud.

ACKNOWLEDGMENTS

I thank my wife Barbara for her love and devotion. Without her and her strong love for God and His Word, I may never have started the long road back to wholeness.

My sons Jared and Joey are the best sons a dad could have. I am so proud of them and who they have become, strong men of God. Daily, they put others ahead of themselves. I am so thankful for their contributions to this book.

To the many people who need God's Word and His "Healing Dirt," please take advantage of both. You are the reason I have shared my story.

More importantly, to my Heavenly Father, thank you for your Word which is the Truth. Thank you for your Son, Jesus, the Word made Flesh. You took me the way I was and did everything necessary to transform me.